MUSTANG

AMERICA'S LEGEND

MUSTANG
AMERICA'S LEGEND

ROGER W. HICKS

COURAGE
BOOKS

An imprint of
RUNNING PRESS
PHILADELPHIA, PENNSYLVANIA

Canadian representatives: General Publishing Co., Ltd.,
30, Lesmill Road, Don Mills,
Ontario M3B 2T6

9 8 7 6 5 4 3 2 1
Digit on the right indicates the number of this printing.

Library of Congress Cataloging-in-Publication Number 90-85928

ISBN 1-56138-024-5

This book was designed and produced by
Quintet Publishing Limited
6, Blundell Street
London N7 9BH

Creative Director: *Terry Jeavons*
Designer: *Wayne Blades*
Editor: *Sarah Buckley*.
Picture Researcher: *Ian Howes*

Typeset in Great Britain by Central Southern Typesetters, Eastbourne
Manufactured in Hong Kong by Regent Publishing Services Limited
Printed in Hong Kong by Leefung-Asco Printers Limited

First Published by Courage Books, an imprint of Running Press
125 South Twenty-second Street
Philadelphia, Pennsylvania 19103

C O N T E N T S

FOREWORD

I first discussed this book with my editor when I was in California, where I live. California, of course, is real Mustang "Road Movie" country.

Then, because of other commitments, I found myself actually writing most of the book while I was traveling: partly in Germany, partly in the Soviet Union, partly in France, and partly in my native England.

What really impressed me was the reaction from people *outside* California. In the Golden State, it was "Oh, yeah, Mustang". Everywhere else, it was "Oh, *YEAH,* Mustang!" Slowly, I began to lose the jaded California perception of the Pony.

I don't pretend that every Mustang has been worth having; frankly, some of them were such dogs that you could teach them to sit up and beg (though they would roll over, or play dead, without any training). There have also been some very cynical marketing games played by the Ford Motor Company, devaluing hard-won names by turning serious performance cars into dull production models. But when you look at the whole history of the Mustang, and discount the worse excesses of the marketing men, you have to admit: isn't a Mustang one of the cars you'd want in your garage, if money were no object?

Roger W. Hicks

INTRODUCTION:
THE ORIGINAL PONY

Ever since its introduction in 1964, the Mustang has achieved the unusual distinction of being simultaneously underrated and overrated. In the teeth of the evidence, some people dismiss all Mustangs because Mustangs aren't "real" sports cars; others, equally misguided, believe that if the Ford Motor Company writes "Mustang" on a motor car, it must be something special.

The truth lies in between. Without question, there have been many Mustangs which were (and are) traditional "hairy chested" sports cars, with bags of power, lots of opposite-lock on the corners, and the same sort of damn-the-torpedos, press-on-regardless performance that purists can only recognize when it comes in the shape of a Big Healey or (preferably) a Morgan Plus 8 – or even a Speed Six Bentley.

ABOVE *The charging Mustang survived two decades and underwent several minor stylistic changes before it all but disappeared from the grilles and bodywork in the early 1980s.*

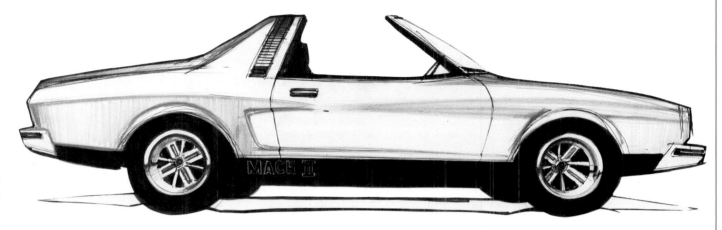

Equally, there have been many more Mustangs which could barely summon the horsepower to pull themselves out of the parking lot and which, even with the meagre power available, still managed to handle like a pig on stilts. There have even been some Mustangs with lots of power *and* handling like a pig on stilts, and in all fairness there have been some gutless Mustangs with very sweet handling. So where to begin?

The most obvious place is with the nature of Ford. FoMoCo is, and always has been, a volume car producer. By definition, therefore, they want to sell Mustangs in volume.

They also know that not everyone wants a fire-breathing, tire-smoking muscle car; there are lots of people who are content with a car that feels a bit more taut and responsive than the old American "land barge", but which still maintains many of the home comforts of the classic boulevard cruiser. The purists may weep into their beer, bemoaning the absence of rock-hard suspension and neck-snapping acceleration; but if modest performance and a sporty image are what sells cars by the tens of thousands, they can hardly expect Ford to refuse to meet the demand. The solution? Easy. Make some Mustangs that the sporting fraternity appreciates; even race them, to show that Mustangs can be taken seriously; and then use the reflected glory (the sporty image again) to sell the less exciting metal.

The other point that has to be made is that American sports cars are necessarily different from European sports cars, just as American cars in general are different from European cars in general. It would be impossible to

ABOVE This design sketch for a later Mustang Mach II serves as an interesting comparison with the first designs.

analyze this at great length, but two factors stand out above all others.

The first is the enormous distances which are taken for granted in the United States – enormous distances, moreover, which are most easily covered on big, flat, straight roads. The kind of nimble handling which evolved in Europe to get cars around centuries-old corners is simply unnecessary in the United States, especially in southern California which has grown up with the motor car (insofar as southern California can be said to have grown up at all). Roads like these, where you may be rolling along for hours on end without encountering anything resembling a corner, require a different style of car from European back roads. You don't *drive*; you *cruise*. This is where the "road movie" image comes from; it's something you can't easily explain to anyone who has not driven in the vast spaces of the American west.

RIGHT AND OPPOSITE BOTTOM Engineer Herb Misch and styling chief Eugene Bordinat created the impressive Mustang 1 in 1962 Although the buffs loved it, Iacocca didn't see the Mustang 1 as the volume sportscar he was looking for and the Mustang 1 was shelved.

RIGHT *Of course, for those who drink their whisky neat (though preferably not before driving), there have been many serious performance Mustangs. The 1985-1/2 SVO (Chapter 7) is most assuredly one of them, even if it is a long way from the raw energy of a '65 Shelby.*

The second factor, which grows to a large extent out of the first, is that Americans are used to big, reliable, simple, low-maintenance motor cars. If it isn't big, you can't take it seriously; it if isn't reliable, it can't handle the distances involved; and if it isn't a simple, low-maintenance design, it is not going to survive the often casual American attitude to scheduled maintenance. An old British expression refers to a lump hammer as a "Birmingham screwdriver", and if a car is unlucky in its choice of owner, the "Birmingham screwdriver" approach may well sum up the maintenance it can expect.

There is one other point to make, too. It is that many Mustang *aficionados* are seriously bogged down in the trim-and-decor side of Mustang ownership; *this* sort of upholstery, *that* sort of color. If nit-picking restoration is your idea of enjoying and appreciating your fine Mustang, but let's not lose sight of the fact that under all the gew-gaws and option packages and flim-flam, there is an American classic which is actually a motor car instead of a rolling extension of your living room. With

ABOVE *This picture of an original '64 and an '84 Anniversary model shows how little the Mustang concept has really changed. It was*

always a sporty looking car, with performance options for those who wanted them, and more suited to being a "personal" car than to being a "family" car.

BELOW *Lee Iacocca believed that fostering in-house design competitions would promote more innovative Mustang styles. This sketch proves he was right.*

ABOVE *Red and white, the perennial theme for Mustang convertibles. If anything, a red body with white upholstery is even more striking than a white body with red upholstery – but the red upholstery is much easier to keep clean! This is a 1989.*

RIGHT *The original Mustang I, designed and engineered by Herb Misch and Eugene Bordinat, debuted at Watkins Glen in October 1962.*

RIGHT *This 1985 5-liter 4V HO was one of the most popular engines and in 1987 gained another four valves.*

OPPOSITE PAGE *The Mach 1, along with the Bosses, took the Mustang range into its second decade. Whilst purists may insist on factory spec paintwork, this customized Mach 1 displays its owners' patriotism.*

the right engine, and the right handling packages, the Mustang can stand among the great sporting cars of the world.

With this in mind, the reasons for the success of the Mustang are not hard to see. It has appeared in many guises, each carefully (and often successfully) aimed at a particular section of the market. It is eminently suitable for American conditions. It is backed by a huge and generally well-respected manufacturer, with readily-available and sensibly-priced parts. It's the star of the road movie. And if some Mustangs are less exciting than others – OK, put your hand on your heart and tell me that a Shelby Mustang *isn't* one of the world's most memorable sports cars.

THE FIRST MUSTANGS 1964-66

Popular wisdom prefers to think of the Mustang's success as the result of accident and not design, and to a certain degree this is true. No one at Ford suspected that they had such a winner on their hands, however, to suggest that the Mustang phenomenon was purely a quirk of fate is to undermine the talent of both Lee Iacocca and his team of researchers and designers. Since the demise of the Thunderbird, Ford had been receiving a steady stream of letters from people, who missed the "personal" touch the car offered. Ford were also casting envious glances in the direction of their rivals, Chevrolet, whose Corvair Monza was selling particularly well. By this time sales of foreign sports imports had reached an impressive 80,000 a year, prompting Iacocca to speculate on the viability of hybrid American car, that combined the flashiness and performance of European imports with American bodywork.

Although no one person can justifiably claim credit for the conception or success of the Mustang, the controversial and colorful personality of Ford's then president, Lee Iacocca, guarantees him prominent position in the history of the Mustang.

Iacocca's philosophy of "thinking young" could not have been more in tune with the time. Market research studies instigated by Iacocca indicated a vast post-war baby-boom approaching car-buying age in 1960. Studies also showed a 40 percent growth in the 15–29 age group between 1960–70, whereas the 30–39 age group would actually decrease by 9 percent. It therefore became evident that any car maker who directly appealed to the

younger market would have a vital and as yet untapped market to feed from. Appealing to this untested market would be no easy task as researchers found strong ideas about style among the American youth. Studies found 36 percent of all persons under 25 liked the "four on the floor" feature. Among those over 25 only 9 percent wanted to shift gears. Bucket seats were a favorite feature among 35 percent of young people, as against 13 percent in older groups. With an 156 percent rise in the number of families whose income topped $10,000 expected between 1960–75,

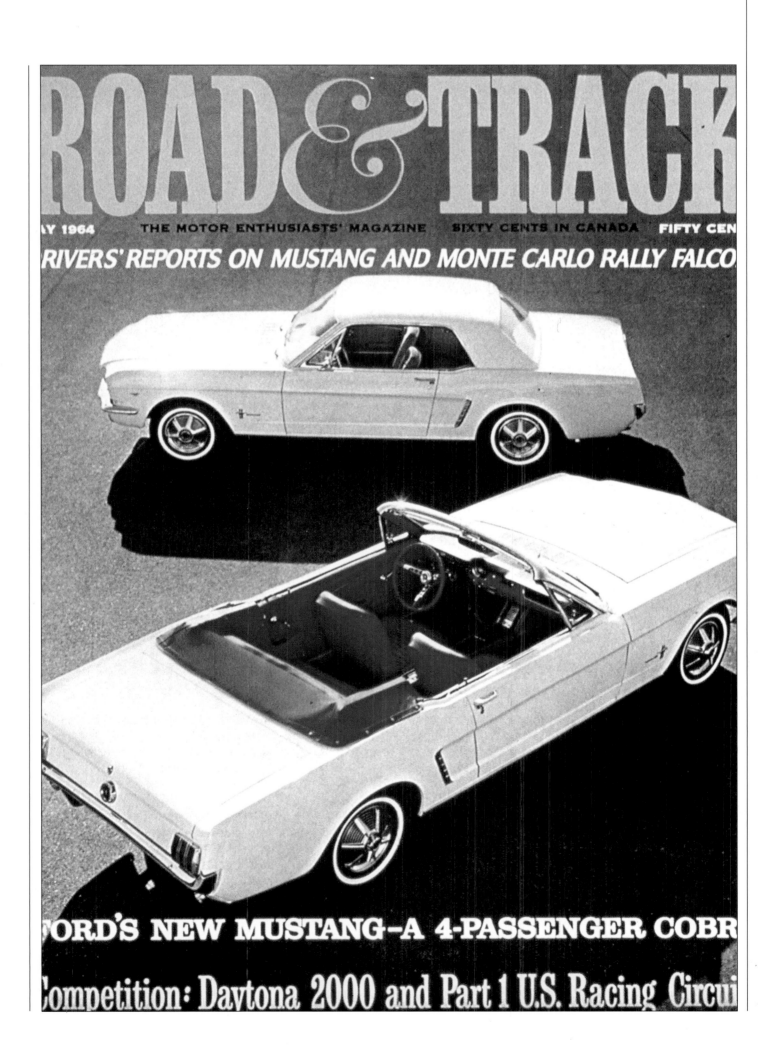

ROAD & TRACK

MAY 1964   THE MOTOR ENTHUSIASTS' MAGAZINE   SIXTY CENTS IN CANADA   FIFTY CEN

DRIVERS' REPORTS ON MUSTANG AND MONTE CARLO RALLY FALCO

FORD'S NEW MUSTANG–A 4-PASSENGER COBR

Competition: Daytona 2000 and Part 1 U.S. Racing Circui

women and teenage offspring were now to be included in car makers' design and marketing plans. The stage seemed thus set for a stylish car which appealed to a younger, more affluent market.

The Mustang I debuted in 1962 at the United States Grand Prix at Watkins Glen, New York, driven by racing driver Dan Gurney. The response was enthusiastic. Car and Driver recorded at the time that it "reminds us of the first two-seat 1100cc Coventry Climax-engined Cooper more than any other car . . . and the Mustang can be more forgiving. It can be braked well into a turn, and with power on, its stability is striking". But this wasn't enough for Iacocca. "All the buffs said, hey what a car! It'll be the best ever built. But when I looked at the guys saying it – the offbeat crowd, the REAL buffs – I said that's not the car we want to build, because it can't be volume car. It's too far out".

Back to the drawing board, and eventually after the XT-Bird and the Allegro, the basic shape, styled by the Ford Division studio under the guidance of Joe Oros, Gail Halderman and L. David Ash, was selected. On September 10, 1962, the Oros design was validated for production and only then did Ford Engineering get involved; the role of engineering was certainly secondary to any styling considerations, and indeed Gail Halderman later claimed he had to "bend something like 78 Ford Motor Company in-house standards or rules in order to build this car". Today, it may look dated: high and boxy, with skinny tires. But in those days, it was an awful lot of things that its contemporaries were not. The squared-off styling was very modern, especially next to the rounded 1950s shapes that were still an everyday sight. The rear fenders had just enough lift to suggest the haunches of a powerful animal about to spring. And while the radiator air intake may have lacked the unadorned simplicity of, say, a TR2 or a Bristol, it was still refreshingly functional-looking when compared with the multiplicity of chromed bars, fangs, and even breasts which adorned other cars.

Ford Mustang Convertible

M·2587

the unexpected...

Mustang hits the starting line full bore!

Here's Ford's new kind of car
no car ever hit the road quite so re
for action. Mustang has a long, l
list of goodies *now*, not six month
a year after introduction. Let's ch
down the list:
1. Three V-8's, from the supersmo
164-hp version with hydraulic lif
through a strong 210-hp two-ba
right up to the solid lifter-header
haust high-performance 271
stormer. And that's not the end;
whole Cobra kit bolt-on array is av
able. (You want the four-Weber

With the car nearing launch the question of the name remained unanswered. Mustang had been used throughout most of the pre-production stages but somehow it didn't seem to stick. Other working titles included "Special Falcon", "T-Bird II" and "Thunderbird II". With Lee Iacocca still

ABOVE *From the start, Ford aimed at a performance image – even if the cars could not always deliver what the image promised.*

se wild one? Just let us know.)

ransmissions? The V-8 choice starts
n the all-synchro 3-speed manual. Or
r-on-the-floor. Or Cruise-O-Matic
ve. All with floor shifts.

What else? A special handling pack
(included with high-performance
s) that makes the Mustang solid as
ullman car on the corners. A Rally
that combines tach and clock
n sweep-second hand. And, just to
w we're versatile, air conditioning,
ix-cylinder saver, power steering

and all the other *dolce vita* items.

We hope we're not immodest, but
the Mustang four-seater starts life with
the kind of equipment and options
most cars take years to come by. And
the kind of rock-solid handling. And
the toughness and durability it takes to
build a going competition machine.

Come down to your Ford Dealer's
and take a long, careful look. If we've
skipped anything that would make
your heart glad we'd like to hear about
it—but what could it be?

For a precisely detailed, authentic scale
model of the new Ford Mustang, send $1.00
to Ford Offer, Department CB 1, P.O. Box
35, Troy, Michigan. (Offer ends July 31, 1964)

TRY TOTAL PERFORMANCE
FOR A CHANGE!

FORD

Mustang · Falcon · Fairlane · Ford · Thunderbird

Although the official launch was to be
April 17 1964, in true Ford PR style the
Mustang had already been released to an
eager public through several orchestrated
"leaks." When Henry Ford's 20-year-old
nephew just happened to drive a black pre-
production Mustang convertible to a
luncheon, *Newsweek* amongst others quickly
snapped up the story. On the evening of April
16, Ford bought the 9.30pm slot on all three
stations, allowing a captive audience of 27
million a front-seat view of the unofficial
unveiling of Ford's new baby. Such an
unprecedented news and media launch
fostered an enthusiastic response and Ford
confidently predicted sales of 100,000 in the
first year. In fact this goal was achieved in just
four months and in March 1966, the millionth
Mustang rolled off the production line.

Again unlike many other cars of the period
– especially those from Detroit – the Mustang
gave the impression that it actually was
engineered, instead of being just styled. The
interior looked functional, especially with the
Rally-Pac with its impressive-looking
collection of dials and instruments; it looked
like it was a machine to be driven, instead of
just a means of getting from A to B.

TOP RIGHT *The
galloping Mustang: one
of the most brilliant
and evocative logos of
all time.*

undecided, John Conley of Ford's ad agency
eventually settled it. At the time he was
interested in horses and had been toying with
the idea of a series, including Colt, Bronco,
Pinto and Maverick. To him at least Mustang
evoked pictures of cowboys and prairies. Plus
in the words of one Ford ad man, "it had the

FOLLOWING IN IACOCCA'S FOOTSTEPS

DONALD FREY GOT LOST IN A SOMEWHAT GIANT SHADOW

In the Mustang's case, history has had a nasty habit of giving all the credit to Lee Iacocca. And while he was the big man who made the big decisions and was responsible for all the really big promotion, many other not-so-big men made major contributions.

When asked why Iacocca gets all the credit, former product planning manager Donald Frey, who made a contribution or two himself in the early going, put it succinctly: "He was my boss". Of course, there was more to it than that, and Frey has certainly not been afraid to give credit where credit is due. Iacocca "had a major role in marketing, creating the whole mystique and the advertising campaign", explained Frey. "And he said to make (the Mustang) a four-seater, which was a key product decision. Up until that point, we had been thinking two-seaters. But he was right; there was a much bigger market for a four-seater".

Frey had been one of main proponents of a new sporty car from the beginning. An engineer who first joined Ford in 1951 as a research metallurgist, he moved over to direct line engineering in 1957. In 1958, he was the executive engineer in charge of the Ford, Thunderbird and Mercury model lines. The following year, he ended up with the Edsel leftovers, then became assistant chief engineer in 1961. Soon afterward, with Iacocca moving up to take the departing general manager Robert McNamara's place, Frey made the jump to product planning manager, and the ideas began flowing.

"It started with a few guys sitting around, including Hal Sperlich and Don Petersen", Frey remembers. "We started watching registrations of the Corvair, which was a dog. I guess in desperation, they put bucket seats and a floor console in the thing, called it the Monza, and it started to sell. We got the idea that there must be

BELOW This design concept Avant/Median, later known as the Avventura 1961/62, eventually evolved into the Allegro II.

something to it". Talk of a sporty car based on the two-seater Thunderbird continued until Iacocca's contribution convinced everyone that a four-seater was the only way to fly – and the rest is automotive sales history. As Frey put it, "that's how it all started – watching Monzas".

In the beginning there was no major market research effort, just "a bunch of guys who fell in love with the idea", according to Frey, "myself, Iacocca, Sperlich, Petersen and some stylists. (The project) was bootleg until late, when we tried to get some money". As for that market research angle commonly mentioned, "they made it all up afterwards – somebody did – in order to sanctify the whole thing. This was terribly disheartening for the staff-types, because it just a bunch of guys – that's how it got started, and that's what we went to market with".

Once a design was finally agreed upon, Iacocca and Frey "took something like five shots with the senior officers of the company to convince them to put money into the car". If there's one thing that Iacocca truly deserved accolades for, it was prying loose the company purse strings, without which the efforts of the other "guys" would have been for naught.

As it was, the money did come, the Mustang did sell and success did come to all involved; Iacocca gettting his expected promotion and Frey moving up to take his place as division vice-president in early 1965. This move gave Frey the rare opportunity of having helped design and engineer the car, while working to sell it too. Though that may not appear like much to the common onlooker, Frey was very proud of his multi-faceted responsibilities during the early Mustang years.

And his pride in the car he helped to create remained strong even after he left Ford Motor Company, as the '64 1/2 Mustang hardtop he continued driving into the '80s attested.

BELOW *Choosing the right color was always important for Mustangs – it still is, for that matter – because some color combinations out of the bewildering choices available are far more effective than others. For convertibles, white with a red interior is still one of the best color combinations today, just as it was when the car was first introduced.*

Unfortunately, with the smaller engine option, it was just a means of getting from A to B: a 101 bhp engine of 170 cid/2786 cc was not going to propel 2,800 lb of car (the approximate kerbside weight) with any great conviction, especially with a 3-speed gearbox, even if the gears were changed by a floor-mounted manual shifter instead of a slush-box. By way of comparison in Britain, Ford's Lotus Cortina had 5 more bhp (from a 4-cylinder engine that was little more than half the size) and was about a third of a ton lighter!

Another great attraction, though, was that there were lots of options. They ranged from the trivial (and merely ornamental) through some useful appearance accessories, such as

almost 160 bhp/ton, even after allowing for the extra 200 lb or so that the big old V8s added to the weight. This was *serious* power: the brand-new Porsche 911 that was just coming into the showrooms offered only about 120 bhp/ton, and the 356 SC 1600 which was still in production was only around 105 bhp/ton. Admittedly, different ways of measuring horsepower (Society of Automotive Engineers [SAE] versus Deutsche Industrie Normen [DIN]) made the Fords look more powerful than they were, but they were no sluggards.

To cap it all, the new Mustang was not only affordable (it started at $2,320.86 for the six, strictly comparable with Ford's Futura, which

styled steel wheels, to some quite interesting performance options – and this is where Ford managed to attract a number of people who would otherwise have been unmoved by just another Detroit styling exercise.

The basic hop-up was a 260 cid (4261 cc) V8 with 164 bhp, while "full house" (at least from the manufacturers – hot-rodders could do a lot more) was another V8 with 289 cid (4737 cc) and 210 bhp. The smaller engine was good for 115–120 mph, the bigger one for close to 130 mph. Instead of about 80 bhp/ton, which was what the six offered, the smaller V8 gave over 120 bhp/ton and the larger one gave

ABOVE *The first "fastback" Mustang was really a semi-fastback, a cross between a conventional "three-box" design and the fastbacks of the future. It was a classic design by any standards.*

suddenly looked very ordinary): it was also offered as a very attractive drophead (convertible) and as a very competent looking hardtop. The 2+2 fastback version did not appear until September, when it immediately attracted many admirers, though some purists felt that the hardtop was a better balanced design.

To be sure, the Mustang had its faults and its crudities. The rear axle, for example, was a big solid beam on cart springs. The 9-inch drum brakes were pretty underwhelming, to the point of being downright frightening if you tried to put one of the bigger-engined cars through the twisties. The 6.50 × 13 tires did not put a lot of rubber on the road, given the weight of the car and the power available from the V8s. The steering, without power assistance, needed plenty of winding: the ratio was 27:1. But all in all, it was a pretty stunning introduction and sales soared.

Whipped to fever pitch by a veritable deluge of Ford promotion, tales of crazed buyers laying siege to show rooms are legion. Ford made optimum use of the enthusiastic feedback from Mustang owners, who literally claimed their lives had been transformed. According to Arnold Grisman, "For the first time a working man's wages could buy a sporty small car with class, and suddenly, a janitor would be transformed, in his own mind, into a suave eligible batchelor about town". Riding high on the emotion, J Walter Thompson copywriters began the "Walter Mitty" ads, based on the character whose rich fantasy life and everyday acts of heroism became their role model. An ad which ran in the November 6, 1964 issue of *Readers' Digest* was typical:

"Two weeks ago this man was a bashful school teacher in a small midwestern city. Add a Mustang. Now he has three steady girls, is on first-name terms with the best headwaiter in town, is society's darling. All the above came with the Mustang. So did bucket seats, wheel covers, wall-to-wall carpeting, padded dash, vinyl upholstery, and more. Join the Mustangers! Enjoy the *dolce vita* at a low, low price".

With America's growing affluence, women were a market which now had to be reckoned with and many Ford ads openly courted the women's favour. On March 19, 1965, *Life* featured the following ad:

"Life was just one diaper after another until Sarah got her new Mustang. Somehow Mustang's sensational sophisticated looks, its standard-equipment luxuries made everyday cares fade far, far into the background. Suddenly there was a new gleam in her husband's eye. (For the car? For Sarah? Both?). Now Sarah knows for sure:

ABOVE *The production version of the 2+2 fastback debuted on October 1 1964. Public demand for the Mustangs reached unprecedented levels and dealers up and down the country were inundated with form orders and impatient customers. One dealer was obliged to turn his show room into an auction room when 15 buyers all wanted the same Mustang.*

ABOVE *Over the years, Mustangs have been available with an almost unbelievable variety of engines. In the first 18 months, there were straight sixes of 170 and 200 cid, and V8s of 260 cid and 289 cid. This is a typical small block V8 equipped with high-performance induction.*

Mustangers have more fun". This rather unsubtle play on sex appeal was further capitalized on in the famous "six and the single girl" ads.

Although the car was introduced in early 1964, the vagaries of the model-year system meant that it was unofficially called a "64½" and officially called a "65" or sometimes an "early 65"; like magazines that come out half-way through the previous month, so that August's magazines come out in July, a new model year begins in August/September of the previous year. It was not surprising, therefore, that September 1964 saw some changes for the 1965 model year.

The fastback body has already been mentioned, but the real interest for most people centered around the new range of engines. The base six was increased to 200 cid (3278 cc) and 120 bhp (around 95 bhp/ton), so that even the cheapest Mustang could just

IT EVEN SMELLS NEW

HOWARD J. EIDE'S UNRESTORED '66 HARDTOP.

Many of today's unrestored Mustangs are flukes which for one reason or another had little use and almost constant storage. Howard Eide of Sioux Falls, South Dakota, has a different tale to tell. The odometer of his Candyapple Red '66 hardtop shows 50,700 miles, and those were logged by the Eide family. They purchased the Mustang in Sioux Falls in May 1966, for $3247.33.

The new Mustang sported the C-code 289 cubic-inch engine, an automatic transmission, power steering, and a Deluxe black "Pony" interior. In late 1975, after much discussion, the Eides retired their Mustang to storage where it collected a film of dust and cobwebs. Several years later it was cleaned and, in February 1983, was entered in an area car show. Much to the Eides' surprise, the Mustang received a Second Place trophy. That first success provided the incentive to purchase a trailer and hit the Car Show Trail.

Since that debut, the Eides have entered shows in Iowa, Kansas, Missouri, Nebraska, Oklahoma, Wyoming, and Minnesota, and have won an average of 16 trophies per season, including two "Best of Show" awards. This unrestored Mustang is no fluke, and its recognition is well deserved. It looks 500-mile fresh instead of 50,000-mile worn. As one fellow enthusiast at a recent show told Howard Eide, "It even smells new".

about break the 100 mph barrier. The 260 cid engine as replaced with a down-rated version of the 289 with a 2-barrel carburetter instead of a 4-barrel, resulting in a nice, even 200 bhp, while reworking the 4-barrel engine gave 225 bhp. This corresponded to around 150 bhp/ton, and well over 160 bhp/ton, respectively.

If you wanted even more power, there was a third version of the 289 which was fitted with a bigger Autolite carburetter, a cam with higher lift and longer dwell, solid lifters instead of hydraulic, more compression (10.5:1 instead of 10:1), a less restrictive air cleaner, and a less restrictive dual exhaust system. To complement this, there was a bigger harmonic balancer, special connecting rods with bigger rod bolts, and other "beefing-up" work. This took the power to 271 bhp, for a power-to-weight ratio of better than 200 bhp/ton – though if you translate the old SAE gross 271 bhp into modern terms, it would probably equate to 230–235 SAE net bhp, or maybe 240–250 DIN. This is still *plenty* of power, and uprating the wheels on the V8s to 14 inches (6.95 × 14 tires) gave the Mustanger more rubber to put on the road (5.90 × 15s were a short-lived option). Perhaps surprisingly, the 271 bhp engine appeared in June 1964, before the 200 bhp and 225 bhp engines, and it remained the leader of the pack.

If you bought the big engine, you had to have the handling package, which was available as an option with the other engines, and you had to have the 4-speed manual transmission. If you had any sense, you would also buy the disc brakes, the quicker steering (22:1, albeit now with power assistance), and the limited slip differential. The styled steel wheels looked good, and if you really were a sissy you could get under-dash air conditioning too. If you didn't load the car up with too much junk, you could expect standing quarters in the fifteens (down from the sixteens for the 225 bhp engine) and a 0–60 time in the sevens, a second faster than the 225 bhp. Then again, the fuel consumption would be in the 13 mpg range, compared with

ABOVE *Six weeks before the debut at the New York World's Fair the Mustang served as the official Indy '500' pace car.*

close to 20 mpg for the six.

The handling package consisted of stiffer springs and shocks, and the Rally-Pac was the easiest way to get a factory-installed rev counter, along with a clock, both of which were (rather improbably) mounted on the steering column.

At the other end of the scale, though, the 200-inch engine was not good news. Like many sixes, it suffered quite badly from harmonic vibrations in the crankshaft. Unlike most well-designed sixes, though, it did not have a vibration damper to help lose these vibrations; and if you really, sincerely tried to extract all of the claimed 120 horses, you stood a very good chance of major mechanical disasters – anything from the flywheel forwards could (and on occasion did) break. The manifold-in-head design was not too good

for breathing, either, so you had the twin drawbacks of relatively poor performance *and* an engine which would, if it was over-revved, prove distressingly fragile. On the other hand, Ford quite correctly assessed that anyone who wanted to thrash a Mustang would almost certainly order a V8, while those who bought the straight six were unlikely to be too unkind to the motor.

So far, everything had gone Ford's way, even if they were not quite sure why. They had a winner on their hands, and there was very little real competition – competition, that is, in the sense of affordable, domestic and sporty motor cars. For comparison, the "big Healey" (the 6-cylinder Healey 3000 Sports) offered almost 130 bhp/ton and 125 mph performance in a much tighter-handling car, but it was $3,635, and even the TR4 with its modest 105 bhp/ton (little more than the basic Mustang six) was about $500 or 20 percent more than a base Mustang.

What was more, the British cars were almost completely devoid of what an American would see as basic creature comforts; we are back to the difference between an American sports car (or at least sporting sedan) and a European sports car. Very few imported sports sedans could match the performance of the bigger-engined Mustangs, especially at a believable price; and among the domestics, Pontiac were still moored in land barges, the rear-engined Corvair was sluggish (apart from the interesting handling), and the Corvette was $4,300.

The Mustang, on the other hand, was fairly awash with both creature comforts and (as has already been discussed) with options. With an option list as long as your arm, Ford PR men could justifiably claim that it was "designed to be designed by you." This was still the America that remembered Kennedy, an America that saw itself at its peak, and an America that loved options.

A partial list – the sort of list that a well-heeled buyer might choose – is most instructive, both for what it includes and for what it costs:

	$
Basic Mustang convertible	2,557.64
271 bhp V8 engine	327.92
4-speed transmission	184.02
Limited slip differential	41.60
Rally-Pac rev counter and clock	69.30
GT Equipment Group	165.03
Styled steel wheels	119.71
Power steering	84.47
Power convertible top	52.95
Deluxe seatbelts	25.40
Air conditioner	277.20
Reversing lights (back-up lamps)	10.47
Full-length console	50.41
Interior decor group ("Pony interior")	107.08
Tinted glass	30.25
Radio and antenna	57.51
Deluxe steering wheel	31.52
Imitation wire wheel covers	58.35
Luggage rack	35.00
Tonneau cover	52.70

This added no less than $1,780.89 to the price of the car (which was itself a couple of hundred bucks more than the basic hardtop) for a grand total of $4,338.53. For which you could have had a Corvette . . .

That people didn't buy Corvettes (or Big Healeys, or other sports cars) instead of Mustangs gives us something of an insight into the Mustang market. For the most part, Mustang buyers were the antithesis of the "no compromise" sports car buyer; they wanted every compromise. If the price of pure performance was minimal accommodations and luggage space, a rattle-and-squeak body with dubious weatherproofing, and the absence of air conditioning, they didn't want pure performance; what, after all, was the point of pure performance to the mass market? Moreover, Iacocca did not intend to build a car for "real buffs."

What the American market wanted instead was a car which looked like a sporting car, and which (with the right options) had at least some of the attributes of a sporting car – most notably, rapid straight-line acceleration. And Mustang certainly delivered.

JOB ONE

STANLEY TUCKER AND MUSTANG NUMBER
100001

T wo weeks before the Mustang's introduction on April 17, 1964, Captain Stanley Tucker, an airline pilot from St. Johns, Newfoundland, was out for a drive when he noticed a considerable crowd gathering at St. Johns' George Parsons Ford. Creating the commotion at the dealership was a Wimbledon White Mustang convertible, a car Newfoundlanders were seeing for the first time. Serving as a promotional vehicle, the convertible had toured Canada inviting America's northern neighbors to buy one of Ford's new ponycars for their own.

When Tucker saw the car, he decided to do just that. He immediately corralled Parsons, sealed the deal and drove away with the white convertible the next morning, becoming not only the first Canadian to own a Mustang, but the owner of the first Mustang as well. Unbeknownst to Parsons and Tucker, the convertible was serial number 100001 – the first of the ponycar breed. Ford Motor Company officials had intended to show off the car in Canada, then enshrine it later in the Henry Ford Museum next to the Mustang I prototype. Of course, Parsons' inadvertent sale to Tucker threw an obvious wrench in the works, and attempts to buy the convertible back from the 33-year-old pilot proved unsuccessful. Tucker was no fool, besides he enjoyed the limelight.

"For a long time, I was the only Mustanger in Newfoundland", he remembers. "It was quite an experience. Many times, motorists would force me to the side of the road to ask me about the car – what it was, who made it, how did I like it and how much did it cost? The car has been a real joy to own and drive. Getting into it is something like slipping into the cockpit, and I feel as much a part of the machine as I do when I'm flying".

ABOVE *This 1964½ Wimbledon white convertible is the same model as the one purchased by Captain Tucker in 1964. Given its classic looks, it is hardly surprising that Captain Tucker held off Ford's inducements to sell the first Mustang for two years.*

exchange for serial number 100001. At the time, Ford was preparing to celebrate the building of the millionth Mustang – what better way to hype the event than to trade Tucker number 1,000,001 for number one?

He agreed to the proposition and returned his convertible to George Parsons Ford in early 1966. "What the heck, there was a new car in the deal", he told *Mustang Monthly* magazine nearly 20 years later. "But it was actually foolish on my behalf when I think about it today". Foolish or not, Tucker made his request for Mustang number 1,000,001, taking the order sheet and marking a large X across the entire page. Except for the 271bhp 289 V8 (he chose the standard 225bhp 289), Tucker's Silver Frost '66 convertible ended up with practically every major option available.

On February 23, 1966, less than two years after Tucker's number one Mustang rolled off the Dearborn line, Ford's millionth ponycar did the same. Then on March 2, Tucker joined division head Lee Iacocca, vice president and general manager Donald Frey, and styling chief Gene Bordinat to pose for publicity photos at the end of the assembly line with Mustang number 1 million, a white '66 convertible. After the ceremony, Tucker was invited to tour the country with serial number 100001, but he declined.

As for the millionth Mustang, it slipped into the dealer network and obscurity. Number 1,000,001 stayed in Tucker's hands for five years until it was sold, rusted and tired, to a St. Johns' mechanic. Its whereabouts, too, are unknown today. At least serial number 100001 remains preserved in the Henry Ford Museum, as originally planned.

Stanley Tucker may regret that deal, but there's one thing they'll never take from him. Though he hasn't driven a Mustang since he sold his '66 convertible in 1971, he'll still be forever known as "The Original Mustanger".

Tucker's enjoyment lasted two years and 10,000 miles, at which time Ford officials turned up the heat in their efforts to get the car back, offering him a new '66 Mustang built to his specifications in

With the big V8 – the K-engine – flooring the accelerator provided the stuff that adolescent dreams are made of. You sank back into the soft seats as if you were in a rocket-ship at take-off. The nose of the car rose about six inches, reinforcing the jumping-leopard styling. The sound of the engine rose from a rumble to a howl, a scream like a dozen Klaxons going off at once, a foot from your ear. And unless you were on dry, grippy asphalt, the chances were that the tires would spin and that you would depart, in a telling phrase of the time, in a cloud of black smoke and rubber dust. Anyone who was inclined to show off in a Mustang was inclined to have heavy rear-tire bills.

Although, the numbers did not reflect the overall feeling of starship acceleration – as already mentioned, zero-to-sixty times were only in the mid-sevens – at the time, this was very good. With firmer, European-style seats; with stiffer suspension, so that the car did not rear up quite so much; and with wider tires – well, the Mustang might actually have accelerated faster than many contemporaries, but it wouldn't have felt as fast, and that is what mattered to Iacocca's intended market.

What is more, many people judged the power of the bigger Mustangs by their ability to frighten their drivers. With plenty of power

BELOW There was not much wrong with the Mustang's styling from its very introduction, as this picture of a '65 convertible shows.

running through skinny tires, and a basically overweight and under-braked car, the Mustang could get very interesting very quickly, especially under marginal traction conditions. The first rains after a Los Angeles summer, for example, turn the roads (especially the freeways) into skating-rinks; and even an ordinary wet road could provoke a Mustang considerably.

In all fairness, anyone who was used to the performance of fast cars of the 1950s and early 1960s could fairly easily collect a Mustang that had stepped out of line; it was a much easier car to drive than, say, the tail-happy Porsches of the time, or even a go-faster Mini-Cooper, which would stick and stick and stick and then suddenly spin with almost no warning. The very high-geared steering made it difficult to drive in the traditional "oppy-lock" style (countersteering, or full opposite lock when going round corners quickly), but you could steer quite well with the accelerator. More power meant more rear-end slide and more oversteer, while easing back on the loud pedal meant that the rear end regained traction and the car was more inclined to behave normally.

Also, the Mustang may have had its shortcomings in absolute terms, but in relative terms it *was* a sporting car when you stood it

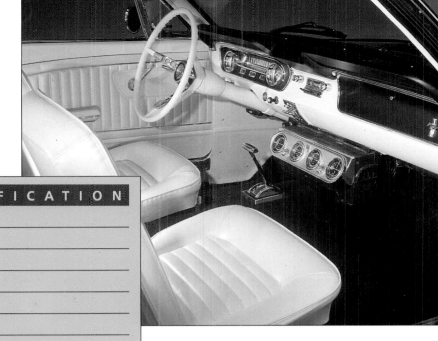

TECHNICAL SPECIFICATION	
MODEL	1965-66 Mustang 289
LENGTH	181.6 inches (4613mm)
WIDTH	68.2 inches (1732 mm)
HEIGHT	51 inches (1295 mm)
KERB WEIGHT	with 289 cid V8: 2860 lb (1300 kg)
WHEELBASE	108 inches (2743 mm)
TRACK	Front: 56 inches (1422 mm) Rear: 56 inches (1422 mm)
WEIGHT	Distribution (front/rear): 53/47
ENGINE	Rated bhp (SAE gross) 210 to 371 Swept volume 289 cubic inches (4736 cc) Bore 4 inches (101.6 mm) Stroke 2.37 inches (72.9 mm) Compression ratio 9:1–10.5:1
PERFORMANCE	0–60 mph Under 7 seconds (271 bhp) Standing Quarter Under 16 seconds (271 bhp) Top speed Over 125 mph (271 bhp)

Note: Performance figures can vary very widely, according to the rear axle ratio chosen, the preparation of the car, weather conditions, and the mechanical sympathy (or otherwise) of the driver.

next to most of the Detroit iron of the day. Besides the market targeted by J. Walter Thompson's ads were unlikely to want the performance sportscar *aficionados* insist on. Most Mustang buyers knew that above average performance was on tap – and they basked in the reflected glory.

Perhaps Ford reckoned that those who knew what they wanted in a motor car would be harder to impress with meaningless gew-gaws. The appalling early wheel-covers (hub caps) were replaced with a flatter fake wire design with imitation knock-ons in the middle; just as much of a gimmick, but a lot better looking. Best of all, on the non-GT models, the Mustang logo "floated" in the middle of the grille, making the front end look still more purposeful. The GT models, though, still used the horizontal grille bar.

Amazingly, the standard engine was still the 200 cid straight-six, and still more amazingly, the standard transmission was the 3-speed manual "crash" box (no synchro-mesh). The other engines were the same variants of the 289 cid as were used in 1965: 200 bhp, 225 bhp and 271 bhp.

As if to illustrate their perception of the car, Ford chose to use the straight-six as the

TOP AND ABOVE Pure performance or creature comforts? The interior of the 1965 Mustangs certainly looked the business.

basis for the first commemorative Mustang, the Sprint 2000, which marked the millionth Mustang. It was a trim option, with wire wheel covers, pin stripes, a center console and (under the hood) a chrome air cleaner with a "Sprint 2000" decal. That was all: no go-faster goodies, nothing. Another manufacturer might have chosen to emphasize the performance character of the car, but as witnessed by the "six and the single girl" copy line, Ford was not aiming at the high performance market.

The majority of '66s sold, as with the '65s, were three-box notchbacks, and the 271 bhp K-engine was *less* common in '66 than in '65, so the rarest and most desirable '66s are K-engine convertibles.

With the close of the '66 model year, though, the Mustang had reached a plateau. Ford knew that GM would be fighting hard for the same market; and although they didn't know what the Camaro and the Firebird would look like, they suspected that the original Mustang would look dated (and possibly also slow) alongside the new GM entries. They also suspected that there might be a serious horsepower race; so '67 saw a new breed of Mustang.

FIGHTING BACK – 1967-68

O nce, a music journalist asked Jefferson Airplane what sort of direction they saw their music taking in the future. There was a pause, then one of the group answered: "From now on, I think that our music will get . . ." The journalist waited eagerly for the answer: ". . . LOUDER!"

Airplane and Mustang are of an age, children of the early-to-mid sixties; and for '67, the recipe for Mustang was certainly "more of the same".

With lead times of between three and five years, the pressure was on the Ford design team to come up with the goodies for 1967–68 before the true success of the Mustang had been assessed. Product planner Ross Humphries later told Gary Witzenburg, "At

BELOW *The 1967 restyle marked a clear transition from the 1950s-influenced styling of the earlier cars to a newer, "harder-edged" style which would continue well into the 1970s. The new true-fastback design suddenly made the older semi-fastback look very old-fashioned; only with the hindsight of a couple of decades or more is it easy to see that they are both classics.*

the time the 1967 was planned, we didn't really have any idea that the original was such a winner. Things did look rosy but we didn't know how long it was going to last". (The Complete Mustang, Haynes 1989).

One thing was abundantly clear, however, and that was that the original Mustang did not receive the engineering attention it merited.

Increased competition from GM (Camaro and Firebird), Chrysler and American Motors (Javelin), also meant that the once empty field was quickly filling up. The competition was also ironically upped by Ford's other divisions with the Torino, a new top-of-the-line series in the intermediate Fairlane line.

Further more, Ford marketeers also didn't suspect that the ponymarket, after a

ABOVE *A rear view clearly shows the indented design of the '67 back end – another "styling cue" from the GT40. It also shows clearly just how high the Mustang sat.*

honeymoon period of four years, had begun to wane. The new Mustang, therefore, had to be bigger and better.

To begin with, the whole car was slightly bigger – a common phenomenon even among the most sporting of machinery, as witness the Jaguar XK120 – XK140 – XK150 progression, or the middle-aged spread of the Porsche 911. It was 2.7 inches wider, two inches longer, just under an inch higher, and about 100–120 lb heavier (just under five per cent). In order to compensate for the the extra weight, extra power was needed; and in order to control a heavier, more powerful car, better handling and better brakes were needed. Fortunately, Ford took care of all this.

The extra power came (inevitably) as an option, a new top-of-the-line motor to supplement the existing line-up. What FoMoCo did was to enlarge the engine bay to permit the insertion of the 390 cid (6391 cc) "big block" engine, with a nominal 320 bhp on tap for something like 240 bhp/ton.

Although the raw figures look impressive, the engine was less so. For a start, it was really a "cooking" engine, with a cast-iron crankshaft, two-bolt main bearings, hydraulic valve actuation, weak valve springs, and inferior induction arrangements despite the 600 cfm Holley 4-barrel carburetter. It was also very heavy (it weighed over 700 lb), and was really more suitable for propelling

traditional "land barges" at a very respectable rate of knots, rather than for a sporting vehicle. The extra weight made even greater demands on the Mustang's already overextended suspension and tires, and changed the front/rear weight distribution from 53/47 to a distinctly less acceptable 56/44.

The wheelbase remained the same, at 108 inches, while the track was increased from 56 inches to 58.1 inches; this made for a much greater feeling of certainty on the road, even with the big-block motor in place. The disc brakes (front only, and still optional) came with power assistance and dual circuitry. The manual steering ratio was quickened slightly, to 25.3:1, while the somewhat dead-feeling power steering ran 20.3:1.

The net result was a car which was adequately quick – the seven-second barrier for the zero-to-sixty time was in sight, but not yet attainable – but which could only charitably be described as sweet-handling. It was just about acceptable in a straight line, but even the Competition Handling Package could not really compensate for the heavy front end. This package, which cost $388.53 in 1966, was only available with the GT option and included the following:
stiffer springs
adjustable shock absorbers (Gabriel)
limited slip differential (3.25:1 limit)
$15/16$-inch (23.8mm) front sway bar
15-inch steel wheels with imitation wire-
    wheel covers
quicker-ratio steering (as quick as 16:1)

For the record, the GT equipment group ($146.71) gave you a typical mixture of genuine performance accessories, useful "go-faster" accessories, and limited trim changes. Serious drivers would welcome the power disc brakes (front only), the stiffer springs, front sway bar and shocks (even without the Competition pack), the wider tires (F70 × 14), and probably the dual exhausts with quad outlets. The grille-mounted foglamps certainly made it safer and more enjoyable to drive at night, and in the unlikely event that you

wanted to race your Mustang, the quick-release pop-open gas cap would have made it easier to fill the tank with funnels and milk-churns. The fact that the tires were whitewall cannot, however, have counted for much with the serious "go-faster" brigade, and the rocker panel stripes were of more interest to "boy racers" than to serious fast drivers, many of whom might have preferred a "Q-car" that *looked* standard but didn't *go* like standard.

ABOVE AND BELOW *The C-stripe on the side of the '68 Mustangs was a "styling cue" lifted from the immensely successful GT40 (based on the English Lola-Ford). The thin bumper is however a real give-away as to the age of the car.*

Of more interest to the average Mustang buyer in 1967 – and much more relevant if you are buying an old Mustang today, when the quickest and most desirable models are fetching vaste sums of money – was the magic word "options", and the fact that the car had been restyled.

ABOVE The big 390 cid engine was something of a compromise. The 271 bhp 289 cid "small block" pictured here was a better-balanced, more sporting engine; but the 390 was the easy winner for the standing quarter.

The overall appearance was still unmistakably Mustang, with the same "styling cues" of a long hood, a short trunk, and the macho rear fenders with the fake air scoop; but there were two major differences, one at the front, and one at the back. At the front, the air intake was much bigger and more aggressive looking, and at the back, the concave rear end echoed (as it was meant to echo) the spoiler-clad rear end of the Ford GT40, one of the ultimate sports-racing cars of all time. No matter that the Mustang and the GT40 were as different as chalk and cheese: when you bought a Mustang, you were buying a part of the same glory, which is (after all) why Ford raced in the first place.

The fastback now became a true fastback. When you are looking at a ratty old '67-'68 Mustang fastback, with the paint chalky and scabby and discolored, wondering whether to buy it, remember two things. The first is that with a gleaming new paint job, that sloping rear end will look a hundred times better – and how much does a respray cost? The second is that the 1967-68 fastback body is at present still underrated, living in the shadow of the convertible. Sooner or later, it will have to be recognized as one of Ford's greatest designs, ranking with (or possibly above) the classic Thunderbirds.

The convertible, with 25,378 models made in 1967, is definitely the rarest body style; but the fastback, with over 42,000 made in the same year, is still not a common body style – certainly, not next to the two-door hardtop, of which more than a quarter of a million were made. What is more, the fastback has more often fallen prey to the tin-worm (which devours the bodies of all Mustangs with considerable enthusiasm) and to boy-racers who wanted a cheap, sporty-looking motor. The net result is that a good fastback, especially with the right engine, is becoming increasingly hard to find – though when you do find one, the price is unlikely to be very high unless it is an original "cherry" or unless it has already been restored.

Which engine should you look for, then? Well, quite honestly, I'd look for a '68; but among the '67s, the availability of the big-

BUNKIE TO THE RESCUE?

SEMON KNUDSEN CAME AND WENT BEFORE FORD KNEW WHAT HIT IT

On February 8, 1968, Henry Ford II shocked the automotive world when he hired former General Motors executive vice president Semon E. Knudsen as Ford Motor Company president. Of course, most shocked was Lee Iacocca, the man behind the Mustang and Ford's executive vice president at the time.

"By 1968, I was the odds-on-favorite to become the next president of Ford Motor Company", wrote Iacocca in his autobiography. "The Mustang had shown I was someone to watch. I was 44, Henry Ford (II) had taken me under his wing, and my future never looked better. But just as it seemed that nothing could stop me, fate intervened".

Knudsen, affectionately or otherwise known as "Bunkie" to friend and foe alike, wasn't the first from his family to work for a man named Henry Ford. In 1921, Bunkie's father, William S. Knudsen, had abruptly left his position in Dearborn and his $50,000 salary behind after clashes with Henry Ford II's cantankerous grandfather, old man Henry himself. William Knudsen then went to General Motors, where he first headed the Chevrolet division and later became president of GM. In 1956, he made his son Pontiac's general manager – at 43, Bunkie became the youngest general manager in GM history, and it was perhaps his youthfulness that helped transform Pontiac from an "old man's car" company to builders of true excitement almost overnight. By 1959, Bunkie was on top of the world as Pontiac sales soared. But when Ed Cole was made GM president over him seven years later, Knudsen resigned in the best tradition of his father, leaving Henry Ford II "with an opportunity he couldn't resist", according to Iacocca.

"Henry was a great GM admirer", said Iacocca. "For him, Knudsen was a gift from heaven. Perhaps he believed Knudsen had all that famous GM wisdom locked in his genes. In any event, he wasted no time making his approach. A week later, they had a deal. Knudsen would take over immediately as president at an annual salary of $600,000 – the same as Henry's".

Seemingly without so much as a pardon me, Knudsen went to work pumping up Ford's image with an injection of GM-style performance. "Knudsen likes performance and dabbles in it, some say, more than he should", commented Chuck Foulger, a former Ford dealership owner in California. "But he knows what the market wants and he knows how to accomplish his goals. I think Bunkie's dynamic thinking is just what Ford needs". Like Iacocca in the early days of Ford's "Total Performance" campaign, Knudsen recognized the sales value of a winning race program. "Any opportunity you have to show off your product in front of prospective buyers is good", he told Robert W. Irwin during an August '68 *Motor Trend* interview. "Racing certainly has a visible effect; our sales increase somewhat every time a race is won".

Probably true, but by 1968 Iacocca and others among the Ford elite were convinced an expensive racing program and high-powered street cars would not lead the way for Mustang into the '70s. "He was a racing nut", said Iacocca, "but he failed to understand that the heyday of racing had passed". Nonetheless, Knudsen ran headlong into the performance market, allotting considerable budgetary dollars for special vehicles manager Jacque Passino's race-minded projects, funding Iacocca had planned on cancelling.

"He (Iacocca) was probably ready to get out of performance", remembers designer Larry Shinoda,

ABOVE *Whilst Ford debated the value of a racing program, "hot rodders" up and down the country took to the track. This 1968 Mustang fastback is seen being put through its paces at the 1969 Winter Nationals.*

himself an ex-GM employee. "Then Knudsen came in and sort of took over, and they pumped in a lot more money. The performance thing was starting to ebb, but Knudsen pumped in new spark. Ford hadn't been doing too good in NASCAR, but they finally got winners. That's where the Boss 429 engine came in; about the only place it did any good was on NASCAR high-speed circuits, because it was kind of a slug in the Mustang".

The Boss 429, the Boss 302 and the new Mustang design for 1971 were all Bunkie's babies. High-powered performance along with high-powered looks were Knudsen trademarks, and the Mustang was just the car for him to show off his flair. In his opinion, Iacocca's ponycar was "a good-looking automobile, but there are a tremendous number of people out there who want good-looking automobiles with performance. If a car looks like it's going fast and doesn't go fast, people get turned off. If you have a performance car and it looks like a pretty sleek automobile, then you should give the sports-minded fellow the opportunity to buy a high-performance automobile". Passino and engineering crew supplied the high performance; Shinoda, who Knudsen brought over from GM with him, supplied the looks.

As impressive as the various Mustang models from the Knudsen era were, Iacocca was openly critical. Even before Bunkie's arrival, he had expressed dislike for the '67 restyle, which basically enlarged the Mustang to make room for a bigger V8 up front. Once Bunkie started adjusting things, Iacocca was truly incensed. "Within a few years of its introduction", he said, "the Mustang was no longer a sleek horse, it was more like a fat pig. In 1968, Knudsen added a monster engine with double the horsepower. To support the engine, he had to widen the car. By 1971, the Mustang was no longer the same car, and declining sales figures were making the point clearly".

Of course, the Mustang wasn't all Iacocca had to complain about. Being the man Henry Ford II passed over, he had good reason to lament when Knudsen was hired in February 1968. "For a few weeks I considered resigning (but) I decided to stay. I was counting on the prospect that Bunkie

would not work out and my turn would come sooner rather than later". It did.

On September 11, 1969, Knudsen was fired. What prompted the firing? "It's obvious, (it) stemmed from differences between Knudsen and Henry Ford", wrote *Car Life's* Charles Malone. "One of these differences was how aggressive Ford should be in racing. Knudsen favored an aggressive program, but (Henry II) and other company officials wanted a de-escalation". Officials also wanted to see Knudsen lighten up a little. Despite a warning in 1968 from Henry Ford II, Knudsen continually stepped on toes and made enemies. Some insiders even thought he was trying to take over the helm of Ford.

As for Iacocca, "the press has often reported that I led a revolt against Knudsen, but his failing had little to do with me. Bunkie tried to run Ford without the system. He ignored existing lines of authority and alienated top people. In the slow, well-ordered world of GM, Bunkie Knudsen flourished. At Ford, he was a fish out of water. Henry had achieved a great publicity coup by hiring a top GM man, but he soon learned that success in one car company does not always guarantee success in another".

In conclusion, Iacocca's answer for Knudsen's dismissal bordered on comical. "I wish I could say Bunkie got fired because he ruined the Mustang or because his ideas were all wrong", he said. "But the actual reason was because he used to walk into Henry's office without knocking. That's right – without knocking!"

With Knudsen out, the door was left open for Iacocca, who joined two other men in a trioka management. Then on December 10, 1970, Lee Iacocca was made executive president of Ford Motor Company. Needless to say, he was far from sad to see Knudsen fail.

"The day Bunkie was fired there was great rejoicing and much drinking of champagne", remembers Iacocca. "Over in public relations, someone coined a phrase that became famous throughout the company: "Henry Ford once said that history is bunk. But today, Bunkie is history".

Eight years later, Iacocca was too.

block 390 dealt quite a blow to the sales of the 289 K-engine, which may not deliver quite as much power as the bigger engine but which offers significantly better handling than the earlier models. Only 472 Mustangs were built in '67 with this engine, making these some of the more desired Mustangs.

Inside, the dash was redesigned for a much cleaner, more modern look which did away with the amateurish-looking Rally-Pac and put the instruments where they were more accessible and the air conditioner was integrated into the design, instead of being quite so obviously a bolt-on extra.

As for the options, Ford offered almost all of the previous goodies, including an Interior Decor Group which did away with the galloping ponies, plus a number of new ones, especially the following:
tilt-away steering wheel
fold-down rear seat (fastback only)
cruise control
glass rear window (for convertibles)
Exterior Decor Group

The tilt-away steering wheel was pretty much what its name suggested and cost $59.93. The fold-down rear seat recognized that the 2+2 layout was more use for carrying luggage than for people, and cost $64.77; an "access door" was part of the option. Cruise control (which required a V8 and a slush-box) was a very reasonable $71.30, and was arguably the most useful single option if you planned to drive for long distances on American roads. Today, with much lower speed limits in most states, the cruise control is even more useful in avoiding tickets.

The glass rear window was much easier to see through than the plastic alternatives which were common at the time, where it was a race between the yellowing and the scratching to see which would first manage to obscure vision completely, and the Exterior Decor Group was exactly what you would expect from its name, a collection of cosmetic flim-flam such as wheel well mouldings and a louvred hood which also incorporated turn signal indicators.

THE BOSS SPEAKS

*STYLIST LARRY SHINODA TOLD FORD A THING
OR TWO ABOUT THE MUSTANG*

When ex-General Motors executive vice president Semon E. "Bunkie" Knudsen joined Ford Motor Company on February 6, 1968, he brought with him more than an understanding of what made GM tick. To the eventual delight of performance-minded Mustang fans, styling wizard Larry Shinoda came along as well. Known primarily for his free-thinking Corvette projects under GM styling mogul Bill Mitchell, Shinoda followed in Knudsen's footsteps, was quickly hired at Ford in May 1968 and immediately made the Boss Mustang his baby.

If anyone can claim an inside track to innovative sporty design, it's Shinoda. After spending World War II with his family in a Nisei internment camp in California, he began his star-studded career by studying at the Art Center College in Pasadena. His first job was a one-year tenure under Gene Bordinat at Ford beginning in January 1955, followed by a seven-month stint with Dick Teague at ill-fated Studebaker-Packard in 1956. With the future looking dim, both Teague and Shinoda jumped ship, Larry interviewing with Harley Earl at GM in 1957. After bouncing from Chevrolet, Pontiac and GM's Advanced Studio, Shinoda went to work almost exclusively on Corvettes, where he remained until his 1968 defection back to Ford. During that time, claims to fame included Corvette showcars such as the Mako Shark and Astro Vettes, the '63 Sting Ray, the Corvair Monza GT showcar and the Z/28 Camaro.

At Ford, his responsibility was to create an image for the Mustang comparable to Chevrolet's Z/28, both in form and function. Although well-qualified to develop the Mustang further was an assignment that seemed a bit odd when you consider Shinoda was among the unimpressed faithful at GM when the Mustang was introduced at the World's Fair in April 1964.

"Initially (we) thought – well, all it is is a Falcon", recounted Shinoda. "Then it started selling like crazy; we said, well we have our Monza. The Monza did sell better than the basic Corvair, but it was still a sewing machine against the Mustang. The Mustang had the right image, and Chevrolet was forced to build the Camaro". That it did – and four years later, Shinoda found himself competing against the highly successful Chevrolet ponycar he'd helped build.

While engineers were dealing with the mechanical end of Ford's Trans Am Camaro counterpart, Shinoda was applying his creativity. Job One involved the name.

"They were going to call it "SR-2," which stood for "Sports Racing" or "Sports Racing – Group II", which I thought was a dumb name", remembers Shinoda. "I suggested they call it "Boss". Chevrolet had already named their Trans Am Camaro the Z/28, but to try and emulate them by calling the new Mustang, the "SR-2"? Well, it was sure not going to help the image of the new vehicle. So I was one of the first people most responsible for calling the new Mustang the 'Boss 302.'"

He was also the guy who cleaned up the Boss 302, deleting the standard Mustang roof pillar horse emblems and the fake rear-quarter scoops. The attractive graphics, chin and deck lid spoilers, rear-window sport slats and wide rims were also his work. According to Shinoda, original plans called for woefully inadequate five-inch-wide wheels on the Boss. "I fought really hard to get some wider wheels", he said, leading to the eventual installation of seven-inch rims.

And the results of his efforts? Shinoda has been more than frank in his comparison of the Boss 302 and Z/28. On the track, the Z/28 repeated as Trans Am champion up against the Boss 302 in 1969, though the Boss would put Ford back on top the following year. On the street, however, it was a tough call.

"I really couldn't say the Boss 302 was dramatically better (than the Chevrolet Z/28)", explains Shinoda. "I've driven both cars, and I don't think the Mustang handled that much better. In showroom trim, car for car, the Mustang was close, but I can't really say (it) was superior". Perhaps the manner by which the Ford people worked compared to their GM counterparts was a drawback to the Boss project, according to Shinoda.

"(They) knew very little about vehicle-dynamics when we (Knudsen, him) came on board", he said. "They never did any testing on a skid pad. Initially they were saying that any kind of bolt-on aerodynamic stuff was bull, that you didn't need it. In fact, they even fought the rear wing because they were saying we've got a big enough spoiler already, which we didn't really have. And the front air dam? They argued about that, too. We finally had to show them how to use a skid pad, and how you develop your vehicle dynamics on it to get optimum handling". Using such tactics, Chevrolet made the Z/28, and in Shinoda's words, it was "one of the finest handling American cars ever built". As for the Boss 302, he could only say it

"was quite good, especially compared to any Ford product".

Improvements were made on the '70 Boss 302, but by the time it hit the streets, Shinoda had hit the bricks. Just as he had come, the famed designer left in Knudsen's footsteps after Henry Ford II fired his brash top executive on September 11, 1969. Shinoda was fired almost immediately afterward. Like Knudsen, he obviously didn't exactly agree with the way things were done at Ford. When aked later what he thought of corporate life in Dearborn, Shinoda said "you could call it conservative, or you could call it some other things, too. They had a strange way of doing things".

After his firing, Shinoda rejoined Knudsen to form Rectans, Inc., a company that designed and built motorhomes. In 1970, Rectrans became part of White Motor Corporation, and Shinoda became vice president of design. When White's design and research department closed down five years later, Shinoda opened his own design consulting firm, Shinoda Design Associates, based on the Detroit suburb of Livonia. Today, Shinoda's projects feature a collection of Corvette ZR-1 conversions.

From Ford, to Corvettes, to Ford, and back to Corvettes again. Is a trend in the making? Only Larry Shinoda knows for sure.

BELOW *The Boss: the awesome 429. Actually most serious drivers in the know rated the 302 more highly but if you had to prove that you were the biggest kid on the block this was the way to do it.*

TECHNICAL SPECIFICATION

MODEL	Mustang 428 Cobra Jet
LENGTH	183.6 inches (4663mm)
WIDTH	70.9 inches (1801 mm)
HEIGHT	51.8 inches (1316 mm)
KERB WEIGHT	3100 lb (1409 kg) approx.
WHEELBASE	108 inches (2743 mm)
TRACK	Front: 58.1 inches (1476 mm) Rear: 58.1 inches (1476 mm)
WEIGHT	Distribution (front/rear): 58/42 approx.
ENGINE	Rated bhp (SAE gross) 335 Swept volume 428 cubic inches (7014 cc) Bore 4.13 inches (104.9 mm) Stroke 3.98 inches (101.1 mm) Compression ratio 10.6:1
PERFORMANCE	0–60 mph Approximately 6 seconds Standing Quarter Approximately 14 seconds Top speed Over 130 mph

Note: Performance figures can vary very widely, according to the rear axle ratio chosen, the preparation of the car, weather conditions, and the mechanical sympathy (or otherwise) of the driver.

Also of interest to restorers (and to students of the English language) is the range of colors available for 1967; the ad-men were as inventive (or as uninventive) as ever, and some of the more memorable options included Frost Turquoise, Diamond Green and Diamond Blue (to say nothing of Clearwater Aqua for those who could not decide between the two), at least four more blues (Acapulco, Arcadian, Nightmist and Brittany), Vintage Burgundy (were we meant to be amused by its presumption?), Playboy Pink (honestly!), and at least three golds (Lime Gold, Sauterne Gold and Aspen Gold). Lavender was at least called Lavender, but what a color to paint a fire-breathing Mustang!

I said earlier, though, that I would rather have a '68 than a '67; and the reason is not hard to find, namely the 427 cid (7-litre) V8 with its racing heritage. As installed, this monster was rated at 390 bhp, but there was lots more on tap if you wanted to go to a private engine tuner. Rip out the hydraulic lifters; change the cam profile; put proper heads on top; install serious carburation to replace the stock 650 cfm Holley; and put in a free-breathing exhaust manifold, and 500 bhp suddenly looked very attainable indeed.

Before you started breathing on the engine, you might have close to 300 bhp/ton; afterwards, you might well approach 400 bhp/ton. Admittedly, you would need to modify the hood and fit larger tires and generally beef up the whole vehicle, but it would still be a very remarkable motor car.

One major drawback was that this excellent engine, probably the finest ever installed in a Mustang, was available from the factory *only* with a slush-box. But if you're going to the trouble described above, you might as well fit a 4-speed manual box, and build the ultimate Mustang. The other major drawback was the price, a hefty $622 over the base model. Given that a fastback was now $2,689.26 and that you would need a *lot* of other accessories such as rev counter, limited slip differential, and every handling accessory you could get, this meant that you could easily spend over $4,000 without buying fripperies and decorations; and if you wanted fripperies and decorations such as stereo radio ($181.39), stereo tape system ($133.86), air conditioning ($360.30) and the Interior Decor Group ($123.86), the $5,000 Mustang was far from impossible.

This may have been why the 427 was officially dropped in December 1967, several

BELOW *The restyled dash was much cleaner and neater than the previous generation, and did away with the Rally-Pac.*

months *before* the introduction of the 428 Cobra Jet on April Fool's Day, 1968. The extra cubic inch wasn't significant, but the engine was a lot cheaper to produce, being basically a production 428 cid engine (a whisker over 7 liters) with trick heads: it added only $434 to the base price, $188 less than the 427.

Whether the 428 delivered 335 bhp at which it was rated or the reputed 400 bhp, one thing is certain though: the 428 delivered bags of power, far more than the average driver could use, and (better still) it delivered it through a 4-speed manual gearbox. There may have been far less potential for extracting more power than there was with the 427, but that hardly mattered: few people were likely to be interested in race-modifying an over-the-counter Mustang, and if you were that serious about race modifications, you were unlikely to feel too constrained by the official FoMoCo catalog.

Other interesting features of the 428CJ included an air scoop on the hood – Ford called it a Ram Air scoop – and "staggered" shock absorbers, at least with the 4-speed manual. These were angled one way on one side of the car, and the other way on the other side, so as to counter the torque reaction of the final drive in the beam axle; they were surprisingly effective in reducing axle tramp or wheel hop under full acceleration, though they were really only a means of "faking out" disadvantages which were inherent in the design. There is nothing to be ashamed of in this, though: the entire history of Porsche cars, for example, has been one of "faking out" the inherent problems of the viciously tail-happy design. Wider tires didn't hurt either (they were F70 × 14 Goodyears on 6-inch rims), but they still were not really wide enough: another inch or two, or even three, would not have been excessive. With the optional 3.5:1 rear axle (alternatives ranged from 3.25:1 to 2.5:1) and a properly set-up engine, standing quarters in the low thirteens were possible, though few production cars could break the 14-second barrier as delivered. The other V8 engines were 195 bhp

ABOVE *This aggressive-looking 1968 Mach I never saw full-scale production. It was used instead as a test bed for the 1969 Mach I. Note the covered headlights and high-mounted grille.*

(289 cid), 230 bhp (302 cid) and 325 bhp (390 cid).

On the ornamental front, styling changes to the body were minimal. Reflectors were added on the sides, to satisfy Federal regulations; the horizontal grille bars disappeared; and the imitation rear brake-cooling scoops were also removed. Changes were made to the Interior Decor Group, with wood-grained plastic on the dash, while the Sports Trim Group got you "knitted vinyl" seat inserts (on hardtops and fastbacks) and a two-tone louvred hood, among other goodies. For the GT group, a C-stripe was introduced which followed the contours of the scooped sides – a modification of the go-faster stripes on the GT40. There were also some regional "specials", such as the California Special (GT/CS), the High Country Special (for Colorado), the Sunshine Special and the Nebraska Big Red. These were trim packages only and not for the serious Mustanger.

By the end of the 1968 model year, though, the "muscle car" wars were really warming up, and Ford knew that they would have to make the Mustang even more brutal in both appearance and in performance; and so they did . . .

THE BOSS – 1969-70

RIGHT *Unfortunately, if you wanted a tachometer, you lost both the oil pressure gauge and the alternator charge gauge.*

BELOW *The Grande was aimed directly at the market then dominated by Pontiac's Firebird.*

The French have a saying: "*Il a les fautes de ses qualites*", he has the faults of his qualities; and this is certainly true of the Ford Mustang. No automobile can be all things to all men. The Mustang did (and does) very well at pleasing most of the people most of the time; but precisely because of this, it has at times seemed somewhat directionless. By trying to fill too many niches, it has failed to create its own niche.

When Semon E. "Bunkie" Knudsen dramatically defected from the GM ranks to assume the presidency of Ford, the 1969 model range was well under way. However, he quickly stamped his own personality on the future of Mustangs, giving the cars a more segment-orientated direction. The rules had now changed, he claimed and the competion was in better shape. With Larry Shinoda now on the design team things look set to improve, with the introduction of the Boss series.

In 1969 the Mustang was restyled again. The wheelbase remained at 108 inches, though the track widened by four-tenths of an inch; the car was almost an inch wider and nearly two inches longer, though an inch and a half lower (achieved partly by lowering the car half an inch on the suspension); and the weight went up by about 150-175 lb.

Although the appearance remained recognizably similar to the previous models, the sculptured side "scoop" was greatly diminished, and the front and rear treatments were very different. Styling changes are always a matter of taste, and some motoring writers apparently like the '69 restyle, but for my money, it was a disaster. The front end was

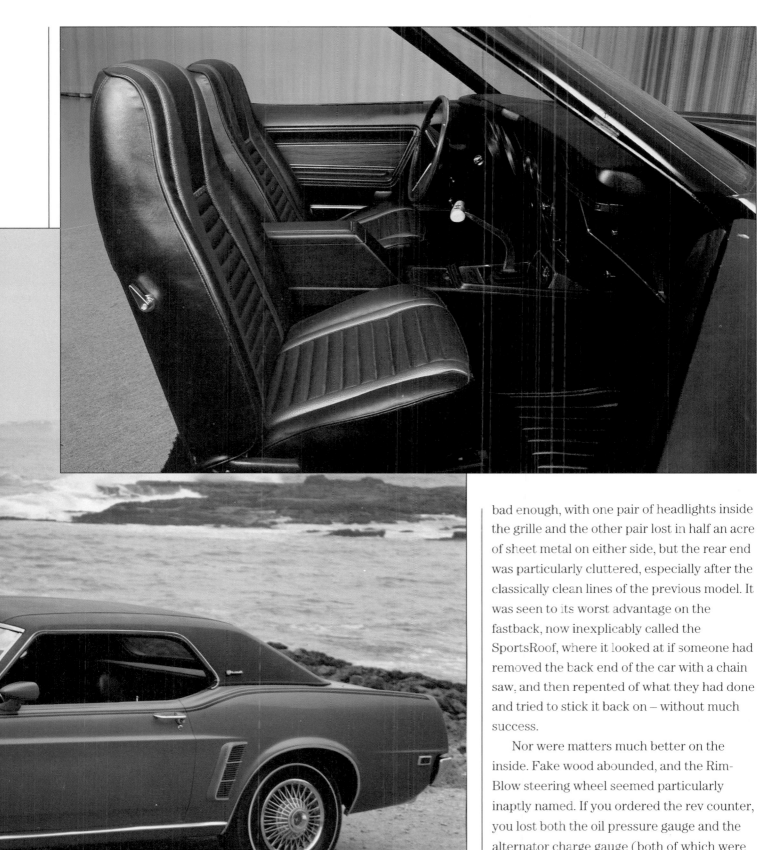

bad enough, with one pair of headlights inside the grille and the other pair lost in half an acre of sheet metal on either side, but the rear end was particularly cluttered, especially after the classically clean lines of the previous model. It was seen to its worst advantage on the fastback, now inexplicably called the SportsRoof, where it looked at if someone had removed the back end of the car with a chain saw, and then repented of what they had done and tried to stick it back on – without much success.

Nor were matters much better on the inside. Fake wood abounded, and the Rim-Blow steering wheel seemed particularly inaptly named. If you ordered the rev counter, you lost both the oil pressure gauge and the alternator charge gauge (both of which were fitted as standard) and had to rely on "idiot lights" instead – what on earth were they thinking of? The Deluxe Interior Decor Group also gave you a clock, but it was fitted on the passenger side where it was almost impossible for the driver to read conveniently.

If the car wasn't already heavy enough for you, there was another option which added 55 lb of sound insulation. With this, and other carefully-chosen accessories such as air conditioning that would sap engine power and add weight, the result was a base Mustang that could barely stumble along: with the 200 cid engine and 115 SAE gross bhp, the power-to-weight ratio could easily fall below 75 bhp/ton.

To counter this problem, a new, bigger six was also made available with 250 cid (4097 cc) and 155 bhp, bringing the power-to-weight ratio back to around 100 bhp/ton; and while the 302 cid (4949 cc) engine with the 2-barrel carb was still around, rated at 210 bhp, there was a new 351 cid (5752 cc) engine with a nominal 250 bhp in 2-barrel form or 290 bhp in 4-barrel form. This was derived from the heavily oversquare 302 cid engine, with the same bore, but with the stroke increased by half an inch – a change in the bore-to-stroke ratio from 1.33:1 to 1.14:1. The top option was a new 429 cid (7030 cc) engine, but we shall return to this later.

ABOVE For those who couldn't afford the Mach 1, there was always the "SportsRoof". In 1970 SportsRoof production totaled 39,316 units.

BELOW The '69 and '70 Mustangs all showed signs of losing their way, at least in a stylistic sense. The front end of many (picture) seemed a bad pastiche of "muscle car" styling.

Bore-to-stroke ratios are interesting because they compare piston area to swept volume. Normally, a larger bore and shorter stroke is associated with a higher-revving engine and more top-end power, while a smaller bore and longer stroke is associated with a flatter power curve and less top-end urge. When bore and stroke are the same, the engine is said to be "square"; when bore exceeds stroke, the engine is "oversquare" and when stroke exceeds bore the engine is "undersquare". Oversquare engines have been the norm for many years, but the 250 cid Mustang engine was actually undersquare.

In practice, power output is influenced by many other considerations such as carburation, cam timing, valve actuation (hydraulic or mechanical), inlet and exhaust gas flow, the choice of cast or forged components, and more; but the bore-to-stroke ratio does give a fair idea of the potential and overall design philosphy of the engine. For comparison, here are the bore, stroke, and bore-to-stroke ratios of a number of Mustang engines:

BELOW *The front air dam on the Boss 302 was actually functional: that is, the car could go fast enough to benefit from a properly designed "apron", and this really was properly designed.*

Swept Inches	Volume cc	Bore inch/mm	Stroke inch/mm	Bore:Stroke Ratio
200 (6)	3277	3.68/93.5	3.13/79.5	1.18:1
250 (6)	4097	3.68/93.5	3.91/99.3	0.94:1
289 (V8)	4736	4.00/101.6	2.87/72.9	1.39:1
302 (V8)	4949	4.00/101.6	3.00/76.2	1.33:1
351 (V8)	5752	4.00/101.6	3.50/88.9	1.14:1
390 (V8)	6391	4.05/102.9	3.78/96	1.07:1
427 (V8)	6997	4.23/107.4	3.78/96	1.12:1
428 (V8)	7014	4.13/104.9	3.98/101.1	1.04:1
429 (V8)	7030	4.36/110.7	3.59/91.2	1.21:1

The contemporary V12 Lamborghini Miura, with an engine heavily influenced by racing practice, had a bore and stroke of 82 mm x 62 mm for an oversquare ratio of 1.32:1.

No fewer than ten engine options were available in 1969, ranging from the "cooking" 200 cid six, through the 250 cid six, and V8s of 302 cid, 351 cid, 390 cid, 428 cid and 429 cid and horsepower ran from 115 bhp to 375 bhp. There was even the "E" (for "economy") model, with the 250 cid engine and a special high-stall torque converter coupled to a 2.33:1 rear axle. The undersquare big six was well suited to this application, and it was very economical for cruising at moderately high speeds.

With the impressive engine line-up, Ford were obviously changing their tactics: 1969 was the year of the performance Mustang. No fewer than three different types of seriously fast Mustang were offered, with three different philosophies.

HOME PROJECT

*DON AND NINA SMITH RESTORED
A '69 BOSS 302.*

This Boss 302 matches its 1969 invoice, and its current state is proof of a painstaking restoration. Don and Nina Smith of Weaver, Alabama, discovered the car locally in 1986. The previous owner had been careful about storage and, wary of theft, had removed the rear window slats and rear spoiler. The original tires were worn out, but the color was correct and only the exhaust manifold heat shield was missing from the engine compartment. A copy of the factory build sheet was found under the carpet.

Nina Smith spearheaded a two year campaign to accumulate correct parts. Don stripped the car, and every part was disassembled or sandblasted for refinishing and reassembly. Various parts were purchased, and those, along with the cleaned and completed parts, were stored in the Smith house away from the dirty work area. At one point there were two bedrooms full of parts, with fenders on a guest bed and the hood in the dining room.

Don rebuilt the Boss 302 engine, and the entire restoration, working in spare time, took one year. Not long after the Boss 302 was completed, the Smiths contacted the original owner of the Mustang. Excited by the Mustang's renewed condition, the gentleman dug through boxes and gave Don and Nina a small collection of original parts. There were five original spark plugs, the never-used ashtray, a jack, and the warranty card. The man wanted to be notified if the Mustang ever were put up for sale. That appears unlikely to happen.

The smallest was the 302 Boss, which was a much better-handling car than the big-block versions, largely because of its better front/rear weight distribution and its lighter engine. To be brutal, it was the only production Mustang where braking and cornering were anything like as impressive as the straight-line performance. The engine was essentially a "homologation special", of which at least 1,000 units had to be sold to the public in order for Ford to be able to race it.

It was derived from the production 302 cid engine, but significantly "beefed up" and fitted with such goodies as a forged crankshaft and forged con rods; 4-bolt main bearing caps; mechanical valve actuation; dual-point distributor; and go-faster cylinder heads with monster valves, no less than 2.23 inches (56.6 mm) on the intake side and 1.72 inches (43.7 mm) on the exhaust side. These saucer-sized breathing arrangements sucked in fuel from a 780 cfm Holley 4-barrel and discharged burnt gases through a twin exhaust. The bottom line was 290 bhp with standing quarters in the high fourteens and zero-to-sixty times in the high sixes, despite a rev limiter set at 6150 rpm.

The Boss 302 was a fairly stripped-down motor car, with a good mixture of "go" and "show" features. The anti-glare black paint that was widely used on the hood and elsewhere was borrowed from race and rally practice; the hood securing pins were as much ornament as use, but at least did not detract from the purposefulness of the vehicle. The front air dam actually helped traction, while the rear "wing" was an option. The functionality of this wing was disputable at any speed, and at less than 100 mph its main effect was to increase drag. In many ways, the Boss 302 is the best balanced of all Mustangs – and given that the Boss 302 engine option added $676.15 to the price of the car, so it should have been. Its main problem is piston cracking, which can occur after as little as 10,000 miles.

You could actually get more power than the Boss 302 offered by buying the 390 cid engine (320 bhp), but as already indicated, this was brute power from an engine that was not really suited for the application. It was also a lot heavier than the small-block. No: if you wanted serious power, and you didn't fancy (or couldn't afford) the 302, your next option was the 428CJ. The extra cost of this engine option was $420.96, though this does not accurately reflect the extra cost of the vehicle because some other options were required, some were recommended, and the chances were (as with any American car of the time) that you would be forced to accept a few options that you did not particularly want, merely to get the car at all.

The 428 was the same engine as before, rated (apparently conservatively) at 335 bhp, but clearly differing in performance according to the options ordered. In its basic form, it came without a functional air scoop on the hood. For $84.25, though, you got the "Shaker" hood scoop, so called because it was mounted directly on the engine (and therefore shook with it) and protruded through a hole in the hood. When you floored the accelerator, a flap in the scoop opened and fresh air was admitted straight to the carburetter. In this form, as the Cobra Ram Air, the 428CJ shaved anything up to a quarter of a second off the standing quarter mile and added a couple of miles an hour to the terminal velocity. Finally, the Super Cobra Jet Ram Air had special extra-strong cap screw con rods, similar to those used on the 427 Le Mans engine, and an oil cooler: these features both allowed high engine speeds to be sustained much more reliably.

Even the 428 Super Cobra Jet Ram Air was second-best, next to the Boss 429. Like the Boss 302, the Boss 429 was powered by a homologation special engine: if Ford wanted to race the new V8, they would have to sell at least 500 such engines to the public in order to satisfy NASCAR homologation regulations.

They were special. The block, superficially similar to other 429 cid blocks, was allegedly cast from superior metal, a hard nodular cast iron. Lubrication arrangements were

RIGHT *The 302 re-appeared in 1970 to much acclaim. According to Motor Trend the new Boss was "even Bossier," and included for the first time in a production Mustang a Hurst competition shifter with T-handle.*

Season after season of Trans-Am wins with specially prepared Mustangs taught us how to set up Boss 302.

'70 Boss 302–Son of Trans-Am.

The Mustang Boss 302 is what comes from winning Trans-Am races year after year. It's designed to go quick and hang tight. The standard specs sound like a $9,000 European sports job instead of a reasonably priced, reliable American pony car. Boss 302 comes in just one body style—the wind-splitting SportsRoof shape. The engine is Ford's high output 302 CID 4V V-8, with new cylinder heads to permit canting the valves for better gas flow and larger diameter. That's what gives you a big 290 horsepower from a small, lightweight 302 CID engine.

Choose either close or wide ratios on Boss 302's buttersmooth, fully synchronized 4-speed. We've made it an even quicker box by adding a T-Handle Hurst Shifter®.

Brakes are power boosted, ventilated floating-caliper front discs. When we tell you the sus-

pension is competition type with staggered rear shocks to combat rear wheel hop on takeoff, don't take our word for it, give it a try. We glue the Boss to the road on 15-inch wheels shod with F60-15 superwide fiberglass belted, bias ply tires. All this leaves you little to option but the fun things — like Magnum 500 chrome wheels, and those great Sport Slats for the tinted backlite. That's Boss 302. Your only problem . . . deciding whether to drive it or "Trans-Am" it.

For the full story on all the performance Fords for 1970, visit your Ford Dealer, and get our big 16-page 1970 Performance Digest. Or write to:

FORD PERFORMANCE DIGEST, Dept. CL-7, P.O. Box 747, Dearborn, Michigan 48121.

MUSTANG Ford

Paint a number on your Boss 302, put a big gas tank in it, and call yourself Parnelli Jones.

supposed to be superior, too, with a 4-gallery lubrication system. The mains were 4-bolt, of course, and the crank and rods were forged.

Crowning this block was a pair of very special light-alloy heads. The advantages of light alloy heads are several, but the two main ones are reduced weight and greatly improved heat transfer and thus cooling. The improved cooling means that the combustion area can be run hotter, and therefore more efficiently. Once again, monster valves were used: these were the days before 4-valve heads, and the

BELOW "Mach 1" was another of those wonderful Ford PR phrases which sounded great and meant absolutely nothing: the speed of sound was most assuredly not attainable, and in any case, the Mach 1 package was mainly cosmetic: the base engine was the less than stellar "cooking" 2-barrel 351 cid engine.

single inlet valve in each cylinder was 2.28 inches (57.9 mm) across, while the single exhaust valve was 1.9 inches (48.3 mm) in diameter. Fuel was supplied by a 735 cfm Holley 4-barrel, the distributor was dual-point, and the exhaust manifolds were very free-breathing. The heads were mounted on the blocks without conventional head gaskets: cylinders were individually sealed with copper rings, while Viton O-rings sealed oil and water passages.

Unfortunately, much of the potential of the engine was thrown away by fitting hydraulic valve lifters and a very "tame" camshaft. For that matter, the carburation could have been more generous, too; the Boss 302 carburetter was rated at a higher 780 cfm than the 735 cfm of the bigger engine. Any serious hot-rodder should have been able to extract 500 bhp from that engine, and Ford should really have been able to offer a reliable 400 bhp or more, rather than the 375 bhp that the engine actually produced; a figure which was, incidentally, confirmed by independent dynamometer tests.

Again, unfortunately, the lubrication of the motor as delivered by FoMoCo was not up to sustained high engine speeds – "high" in this

TECHNICAL SPECIFICATION	
MODEL	1969 Boss Mustang 302
LENGTH	187.4 inches (4760 mm)
WIDTH	71.8 inches (1842 mm)
HEIGHT	50.3 inches (1278 mm)
KERB WEIGHT	3300 lb (1500 kg) approx.
WHEELBASE	108 inches (2743 mm)
TRACK	Front: 58.5 inches (1486 mm) Rear: 58.5 inches (1486 mm)
WEIGHT	Distribution (front/rear): 56/44
ENGINE	Rated bhp (SAE gross) 290 Swept volume 302 cubic inches (4949 cc) Bore 4 inches (101.6 mm) Stroke 3 inches (76.2 mm) Compression ratio 10.5:1
PERFORMANCE	0–60 mph Under 7 seconds Standing Quarter Under 15 seconds Top speed Over 120 mph

Note: Performance figures can vary very widely, according to the rear axle ratio chosen, the preparation of the car, weather conditions, and the mechanical sympathy (or otherwise) of the driver.

case meaning over 6000 rpm, despite the 8000 rpm tachometer. The result was the car ran its bearings with distressing frequency. Once again, independent hot-rodders have solved this problem, but on a Mustang that cost well over $4,000 in basic form, such problems should not really have arisen.

On the other hand, unlike the 428 Mustangs, the Boss 429 was much more than a big engine stuffed into a medium-sized car. As with the Boss 302, the suspension was significantly modified to improve handling and the track was wider than the standard Mustang. The wheels were Magnum 500s, fitted with Goodyear F60 × 15 tires, so there was more rubber on the road. Sway bars were fitted at both front and rear (this was the first Mustang with a rear sway bar). With the battery re-located in the trunk, weight distribution was somewhat improved, though the front was still heavy and the rear-mounted battery did nothing for the polar moments of inertia. Incredibly, given that the engine alone was an option which cost $1,208.35, it cost another $32.44 to have the battery moved, and the front air dam was an option at $13.05.

A total of 899 Boss 429 Mustangs were built, and not all of those have survived. They are certainly rare, and they are regarded by many as the ultimate performance Mustang.

To return to the more pedestrian Mustangs, a new designation appeared to describe the Mustang performance image (as distinct from actually making the car go faster): the Mach 1. The Mach 1 option was essentially cosmetic: a hood painted flat black, with a fake air scoop and optional NASCAR-style retaining pins; reflective side and tail stripes; a chrome pop-open gas cap

and a bevy of features to delight the purist and dedicated restorer alike, such as body-colored racing mirrors. There was also a modest "competition suspension" option (standard with the Mach 1, otherwise $30.64) with stiffer springs, heavier-duty shocks, a bigger front sway bar and (if you specified the 4-speed box) staggered shocks. The standard engine for the Mach 1 was the 351 2-barrel, with the bigger (but not smaller) engines as options. The GT option remained available as a slightly less flashy decoration pack, again with the improved suspension. However, this sold in far smaller numbers.

Another option was the so-called Grande (which wasn't any bigger, demonstrating the fact that they don't speak much Spanish in Dearborn) but which was rather more luxurious and had the aforementioned 55 lb of sound deadening material as standard. It was available only in the hardtop.

For 1970, the styling was cleaned up. The front end was much less cluttered, with both pairs of lamps inside the grille area. The rear end looked slightly less amateurish, and the vestigial imitation scoops mounted high on the rear wing disappeared. The Mach 1 hood was no longer flat black; the GT option disappeared altogether. The Shaker scoop was now available on all V8s of 351 cid and above, while the rear wing could be ordered for any hardtop, even with the 200 cid engine. There were all sorts of detail changes, mostly pretty marginal, such as the so-called "Grabber" roof, which was simply a special paint job. Otherwise, it was pretty much The Mixture As Before, which is why this book is divided up as it is; it would be 1971 before the Mustang saw another major restyle.

THE LAST OF THE OLD GUARD – 1971-73

According to a January, 1971, Mustang ad, "'71 Mustang. New style and handling from a Trans Am winner." And indeed the 1971 Mustang looked – and was – bigger than any Mustang so far. The wheelbase grew for the first time, though only by an inch to 109 inches. The overall length increased by 2.1 inches, the width by 2.3 inches, and the track by a welcome 3 inches. The huge hood was much

BELOW The biggest-looking, meanest-looking Mustangs yet: the last of the first generation. The ultra-"clean" rear end treatment is very clear in this picture while the striping is more open to aesthetic dispute. This is, moreover, a Boss 351, the new Boss Mustang for the 1971 model year.

wider than anything seen so far on a Mustang, and the front end treatment was greatly simplified. At the back, there was a welcome return to the simplicity of the 1969 fastback treatment, though the scooped reverse-curve rear window of the hardtop coupé was not the most successful example of that type of styling; the Jaguar XJ-S, for example, did it much better. It is only fair to say, too, that while the big, flat rear window of the fastback

looked good and was aerodynamically quite effective, it was also difficult to see out of unless it was sparkling clean. Given that it was only 14 degrees from the horizontal, this is hardly surprising!

At long last, the 200 cid engine was dropped (retaining it would have meant worse than 70 bhp/ton), and the undersquare 250 cid engine became the base power unit, rated at 145 bhp. There were still plenty of other engine options, though: a 210 bhp version of the old faithful 302, a 351 in four versions from 240 bhp to 330 bhp, and a 429 rated at either 370 or 375 bhp. Both the 302 and the 429 Boss Mustangs were dropped, to be replaced by the Boss 351: a change in NASCAR regulations meant that the 351 cid engine could be raced, and (as before) the road-going Boss Mustang engine was derived from racing practice.

To start at the fun end, the 429 was Ford's most recent big block design, introduced in the Thunderbird 1968 and used (in heavily modified form) in the 429 Boss. It was also made in a 460 cid version (7538 cc) for the big Lincolns, and apparently there was room to provide a swept volume of 501 cid (8210 cc), though this never materialized as a result the of the "gas crisis".

Despite very large valves in the two-valve-per-cylinder heads, 4-bolt main caps, and an an 11.3:1 compression ratio, the 429CJ and 429CJ-R (ram-air) engines were still severely handicapped by hydraulic valve actuation and inadequate carburation (700 cfm Rochester Quadrajet). The 429CJ-R added only $436.00 to the price of the car, though. This time, too, Ford did some of the hot-rodders' work for them: the 429SCJ-R ("Super" CJ-R) had mechanical valve actuation, a Holley 780 cfm carburetter, and forged pistons – though an oil cooler remained an option.

You could tell the market the 429SCJ-R was aimed at: it was available only with the Drag Pack, which consisted of a limited slip differential by either Traction-Lok ($155.00) or Detroit Locker ($207.00), so straight-line performance was the name of the game.

ABOVE *The theory behind this sort of rear window, and the reason why it is found on seriously fast cars, is that the extended roofline moves the center of pressure backwards and thereby improves the high speed stability.*

Fewer than 2000 Mustangs were built with the big engines, and fewer than one third of those had the 429SCJ-R. Either the 4-speed manual or the C-6 automatic could be specified.

Never mind. The new car looked good, and even if power-to-weight ratios were not in the same class as the Boss 429, the bigger-engined models went very fast in a straight line. If you wanted something more advanced – such as, for example, the ability to turn corners – you might be better served by the new Boss, the 351. As already mentioned, revised NASCAR rules allowed engines of this capacity, and making a single Boss with this engine was very much more economical cheaper than making the two Boss Mustangs of yore. The engine was less special than the previous offerings, but it was still good stuff: mechanical valve actuation, an 11:1 compression ratio, forged rods, selected cranks, 4-bolt mains, and a 750 cfm Motorcraft carburetter.

As before, the Boss package meant much tighter handling, and the Boss 351 was arguably the sweetest of the Boss series with plenty of low-end power (because of the longer stroke when compared with the 302)

and a very fair top-end. It was rated at 330 bhp, but given that it weighed no less than 3750 lb but could still cover the standing quarter mile in around 14 seconds (some were a little better, some a little worse), most people reckoned that Ford were, for their own inscrutable reasons, being economical with the truth concerning the power of this engine. The Boss 351 cost $4,124, compared with $2,911 for the basic two-door hardtop coupé with the cooking 250 cid six, but that got you a front air dam and all kinds of other goodies as well as the engine and suspension improvements.

Moving down again, the regular Mach 1 with the 4-barrel 351 still gave you 285 bhp, while the 2-barrel was rated at 240 bhp. Power-to-weight figures are instructive, though: just under 180 bhp/ton for the 4-barrel, just over 150 bhp/ton for the 2-barrel. All Mach 1 Mustangs came with the hopped-up suspension and 7/8 inch front and 1/2 inch rear sway bars, unless you bought the 429 engine, in which case the rear sway bar was 5/8 inches. You could actually buy a Mach 1 with the 302 cid engine, though you would need to be either unusually careful with the pennies, or possibly somewhat unclear on the concept of fast cars, in order to do so: 132 bhp/ton is not much, especially given the sheer inertia of the 1971 Mustang.

Given the original tires, though, you might not want too much performance; the handling of most Mustangs at the limit has always been distinctly interesting, though the Boss versions did expand the performance envelope a bit. Modern, stickier tires will mean that it takes much longer to lose control of a Mustang, but when you do, you will have your hands full.

Because it was a Mustang, you didn't necessarily have to buy more performance than you wanted, merely to get the go-faster look. During the 1971 model year, first Boss-style "performance" graphics were available on the Mach 1, and then a Sports Hardtop was made available with a Mach 1 grille, NASA hood, Boss 351-style side-stripes, and more. You could order this even with the base engine, so (once again) Ford was selling reverse Q-cars, Mustangs which looked a lot faster than they were.

If you've ever wondered about the term Q-car, incidentally, it is borrowed from the World War 2 practice of arming merchant ships and then concealing the guns. A submarine would rarely waste a torpedo on an unarmed merchantman, but would surface to sink her by gunfire. Once the U-boat was well and truly on the surface, the merchantman would uncover her guns and sink the submarine instead. Such ships were called Q-ships.

In 1972, the Mustang was obviously on the way out. There were no body changes. The big-block option with the 429 cid engine disappeared, and so did the Boss 351. For a little while, there was a 351 HO (for "High Output") engine, which was basically a Boss 351 with a lowered compression ratio (8.8:1) so that it would run on regular fuel instead of the high octane gas that the Boss required. The fortunate owner of one of these rare cars (around 1000 were built – the engine was available in any body style) still has 275 bhp SAE net (probably more than 300 bhp under the old SAE gross rating) under his foot, for zero-to-sixty times in the mid-to-high sixes and standing quarters of just over 15 seconds with a terminal velocity of 95+ mph. These were the last true performance Mustangs, and required options included power front discs, Competition suspension, a 4-speed manual box, wide tires on 15-inch wheels and a limited slip differential. Reducing the compression ratio of the engine also made it even more tractable, so the fact that the gearbox had widely-spaced ratios was no great disadvantage.

Otherwise, the engine options were the 4-barrel 351CJ, with a very respectable 266 bhp SAE net; the 2-barrel 351C with 177 bhp; the 2-barrel 302 with 140 bhp; and the 250 straight-six with a mere 98 bhp. These lower figures reflect two things: lowered

BELOW *This view of the 351 Boss clearly shows the billiard-table-sized hood, with its seemingly endless expanse of matte black and its very clean front-end styling, complete with front spoiler.*

GENUINE SURVIVOR

When Bill Johnson saw the 1971 convertible in 1983 he overlooked the fact that the car had suffered five previous owners, a dashboard fire, an "attempted" restoration, trunk floor rust holes and abandonment under a tree near salt water. Under the rust he saw a lovely red roadster.

A first-time restorer, Bill was pleased with his new purchase. Never mind the bent top bows and rotted shock towers. The incorrect paint and foot level ventilation were not problems. The engine and transmission were correct, and Bill Johnson thought it was "a marvellous car. A little bit of this, and a little bit of that" would make it right.

Bill's double whammy consisted of a visit to a large Mustang show and the purchase of *"How To Restore Your Mustang"*. That's when he realized he had violated Rule One, "Never buy a piece of junk". Larry Palmer, an experienced body man in Redmond, walked him through enough repairs "to buy the Brooklyn Bridge". New shock towers, rear quarter panels, front fenders, trunk metal, a door, and two new floor pans would do it. Still, Bill decided to commence the restoration. It would take three years to reach completion.

In planning his expenditures, Johnson had two goals. He chose to stay Mustang-original, but he also chose to add options not included on the red convertible's factory build sheet. When new the car had only a radio, power steering, brakes, and top, and tinted glass. Bill decided to add the Decor Group, Instrumentation Group, and Convenience Group, as well as a NASA hood, Magnum 500 wheels, space saver spare tire, AM-FM radio, dual exhaust, power windows, and intermittent wipers.

When Larry Palmer had finished the body work, the Mustang was moved to All-Tech in Issaquah where Chris Le-Boutillier and Fred Malmassari applied Sikkens paint in original Bright Red. Fellow Mustangs Northwest member Rene White of Arlington, Washington, rebuilt the transmission, Jim's Automotive in Redmond overhauled the

engine, and Bill undertook his own upholstery, power window installation, and engine compartment and undercarriage detailing. Correct hoses and other Autolite items were installed, all chrome and stainless parts were refinished or replaced, and Dixon Swank of Spatz Detailing advised in the final touches.

Since 1987 Bill Johnson's convertible has never taken less than a First Place award, including the San Diego Sea World show that year, and the '89 MCA-sanctioned show in Hollywood, California. It also won twin Best of Show Trophies at the huge Mustangs Northwest Round-Up in Bellevue, Washingon, and in September at the Greater Vancouver Mustang Association Show. So, despite breaking the first rule of Mustang restoration, Bill Johnson has both a winner and roadster able to grace any boulevards.

TECHNICAL SPECIFICATION

MODEL	1971 Boss Mustang 351
LENGTH	189.5 inches (4813 mm)
WIDTH	74.1 inches (1882 mm)
HEIGHT	50.1 inches (1273 mm)
KERB WEIGHT	3750 lb (1705 kg) approx.
WHEELBASE	109 inches (2769 mm)
TRACK	Front: 61.5 inches (1562 mm) Rear: 61.5 inches (1562 mm)
WEIGHT	Distribution (front/rear): 56.5/43.5
ENGINE	Rated bhp (SAE gross) 330 Swept volume 351 cubic inches (5752 cc) Bore 4 inches (101.6 mm) Stroke 3.5 inches (88.9 mm) Compression ratio 11.7:1
PERFORMANCE	0–60 mph Just over 6 seconds Standing Quarter Approximately 14 seconds Top speed Over 125 mph

Note: Performance figures can vary very widely, according to the rear axle ratio chosen, the preparation of the car, weather conditions, and the mechanical sympathy (or otherwise) of the driver.

compression ratios, necessary to deal with lower-octane regular gas, and a considerable revision of bhp rating practices.

Formerly, engines were measured "gross", with no ancillary equipment installed and running under the most favorable conditions on a test bed – and the test procedure was open to interpretation. The new SAE net rating system attempted to measure the power of the engine in something more like operable form. The result was a significant drop in power ratings: where SAE ratings had typically run 10-20 per cent *above* DIN standards (*Deutsche Industrie Normen*, the rigorously-defined German industry standard), they now started to run about five percent *below* DIN standards.

Moving from "go" to "show", a cynic might have found the Sprint paint option to his

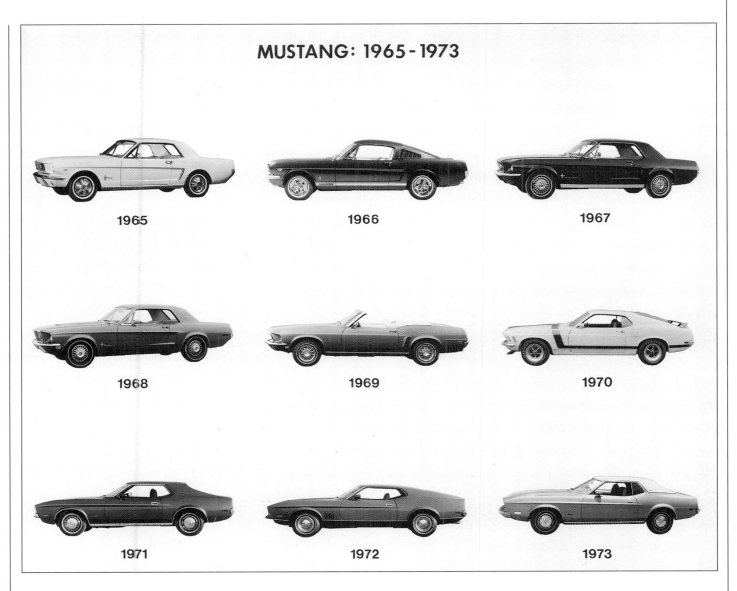

MUSTANG: 1965-1973

1965

1966

1967

1968

1969

1970

1971

1972

1973

ABOVE *The all-star line-up spanning 1965–73 gives a pretty good idea of how the Mustang evolved to keep up with (and sometimes even ahead of) the times, throughout its first incarnation.*

LEFT *Sprint Decor options for the 1972 Mustang played on American patriotism in an attempt to boost sales. Red and blue highlights accompanied USA decals at the rear.*

liking. In a year when the Mustang was obsolescent and waning in power, the Sprint had a red, white and blue paint job with a "US" shield decal on the rear quarter panel. Evidently, Ford had decided to reverse a well-known presidential dictum, and to talk loudly while carrying a small stick.

The 1973 model year was even more of a disappointment. The front grille was slightly changed, neither for better nor for worse; the color-keyed front bumper was designed to resist the mandatory 5 mph crash testing; and (as Peter Sessler points out in his Mustang Buyer's Guide), a 1965 Mustang with the 289 cid engine would out-accelerate the quickest 1973 Mustang available.

As the 1973 model year drew to a close, the Pony had almost completely lost its direction. It looked broader and sleeker than

the original, but it was 800 lb heavier – an increase of well over 25 percent. Even by American standards, it was no longer small and light and therefore no longer sporty. It had such features as concealed wipers, definitely *not* essential on a sporting car.

Having now deviated substantially from the original Mustang, Ford no longer appealed to the true Mustang market. It was still selling quite well, but sales were on the wane: 134,867 Mustangs were built in 1973, better than the 125,093 of 1972 (the worst year so far), but still a long way down on the 607,568 of 1966 or even the 317,404 of 1968. The only possibility was a serious redesign. What emerged was a completely different car from its predecessors, and one which (despite its merits) all but destroyed the Mustang name.

MUSTANG II
— 1974-78

With Lee Iacocca back at the Ford helm, things looked set to improve again after a period of mediocre sales. Iacocca was one of the few who believed that a market still existed for the original Mustang. "When I look at the foreign-car market and see that one in five is a sportscar, I know something is happening. Look at what the Celica started to do before two devaluations nailed it. Anyone who decides to sit this out just ain't gonna dance", he proclaimed. By now the Mustang was anything but the cheap, sporty-looking car it had been in 1964. Moreover, even the fastest Mustang was a long way from performance-car speeds. From being all things to all men it had evolved to a point where it was nothing to anyone. So the design team

were urged to go back to basics. Original plans to develop a 'fat' Mustang were quickly shelved when the bottom dropped out of the ponycar market. Iacocca remained unimpressed with the 'Ohio" and "Arizona" prototype models, and once again Iacocca held an in-house competition to design the new Mustang according to his parameters: "The new Mustang must be small, with a

ABOVE *The interior of the Mustang II was cleaner than its predecessors.*

LEFT *Aimed at the sporty import coupe market, the 1974 Mustang II shed 20 inches in length and 13 inches in wheelbase.*

OPPOSITE PAGE BOTTOM *The Ghia range continued in 1974 where the Grandes had begun, ie top of the range. For an additional $199 you could also buy a V-8 engine.*

wheelbase of between 96 and 100 inches. It must be a sporty notchback and/or fastback coupe; the convertible is dead and can be forgotten . . . Most important, it must be luxurious – upholstered in quality materials and carefully built".

He got what he wanted. The wheelbase shrank by well over a foot, from 109 inches to 96.2 inches. The track dropped almost 6 inches at the front, a little less at the rear (55.6 inches/55.8 inches), a whisker less than the 56/56 inches of the original car. The length dropped more than half a yard, to 175 inches (6.6 inches shorter than the original model), the width fell by just under 4 inches (though it was still nearly 2 inches wider than the original model), and the height was only two-tenths of an inch less than the preceding model. Depite all this, the weight of the new car, rated "sub-compact",

stayed around 2,700 lb before you started adding weighty options.

The engineers and designers had miscalculated as there was nothing like enough power to propel this undersized, overweight car. The base engine was a 140-cid (2.3-liter) in-line four delivering a meagre 88 bhp – just over 70 bhp/ton, ready to roll. The new four was America's first all-metric engine, with a cross-flow single overhead cam head, but the specific power output was an appalling 38 bhp/liter, and it was really too big for a four (straight fours of more than 2 liters are inclined to be lumpy, unless fitted with balance shafts). This was why it had to be mounted in a subframe, to isolate it from the rest of the (unitary) chassis.

The only other engine option was not much better: the German-built 171 cid (2.8 liter) V6 was undoubtedly smoother than the four, but the 105 bhp that it delivered in American trim was most certainly nothing to write home about. At best, you might have rather better than 80 bhp/ton; with a "full house" Ghia body and all the options, you would probably drop to about 70-75 bhp/ton again, certainly unworthy of the Mustang name.

There was worse to follow: there were no convertibles, only hardtop coupés and fastbacks. The fine old body-building name of Ghia, which Ford had acquired in 1970, was simply prostituted in a piece of "badge engineering" designed to lend some sorely-needed prestige to the luxury version of the Mustang II, the replacement for the Grande. The body itself still had a faintly Mustang air to it, with a long (-ish) hood and a short (-ish)

ABOVE *The fastback Mach 1 pictured here cost $3,674 and included 170 cid V6 engine.*

deck, within the considerable limitations imposed by the downsizing, and the dreaded side-scoops reappeared; all in all, it could not be called a handsome car.

On the bright side, the new rack and pinion steering was very much better and more precise than the old recirculating-ball type; disc brakes were (at long last) standard on the front; the front suspension gave a better ride *and* better handling; and the wildly outdated 3-speed crash gearbox was replaced with a 4-speed synchromesh box as the base option. Alloy wheels were available as an option, though they would have been much more useful on the old "muscle" Mustangs.

Fortunately for Ford, the new car was launched just as people began to believe that there would never be enough gas again. The "gas crisis" of 1973 was part real, part hysterical (there were tankers standing offshore, not allowed to unload their cargo to waiting refineries), and a panicked public turned their backs on gas guzzlers: the Mustang II was small and (relatively) economical, and it was therefore snapped up to the tune of just under 386,000 cars.

LEFT *More of the same was definitely the recipe for 1977; as this picture shows there was little development from the 1974 Mustangs. However, an already extensive options list grew to encompass an anti-theft system, electric rear-window defroster and several new sound systems.*

ABOVE *Faced with declining sales and stiffer competition, Ford reverted to the old 'Mustang' appelation.*

LEFT *The option package for the 1978 King Cobra included a brushed-aluminium instrument panel appliqué as pictured here.*

OVERLEAF *Only 500 "king-of-the-road" King Cobras were ever built, making them some of the most sought-after Mustangs.*

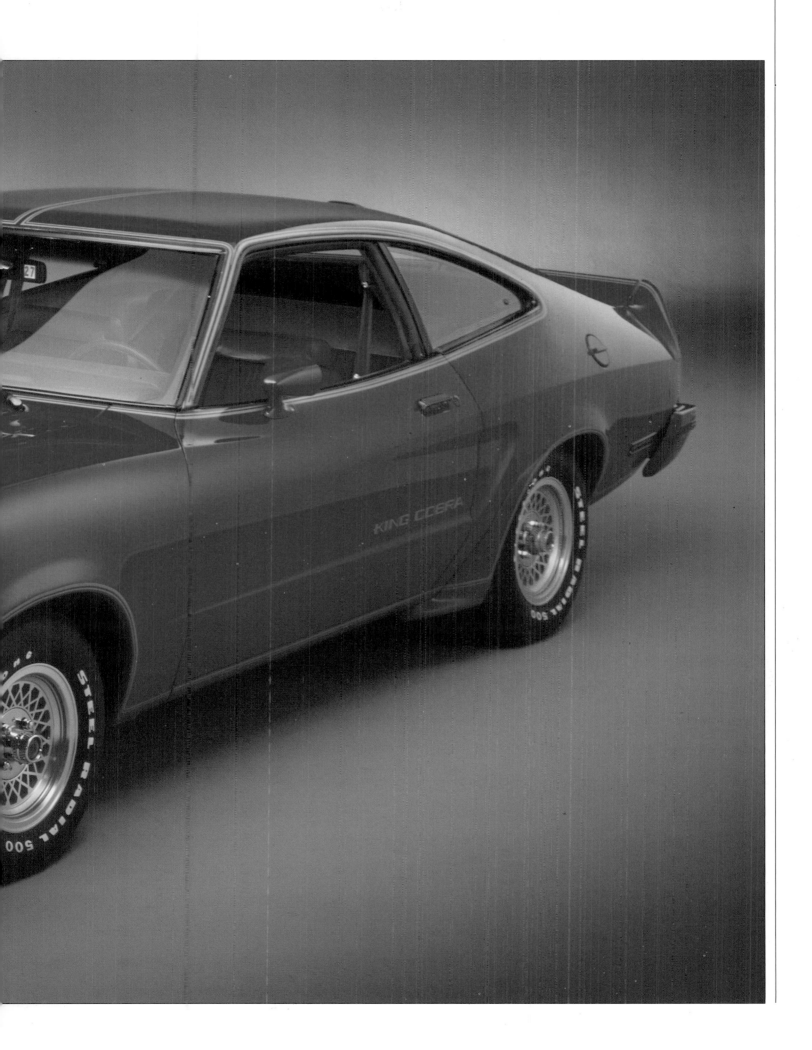

For 1974, Ford revived the Mach 1 name when they fitted a 302 cid V8 – though this was almost as much of a betrayal as the Ghia badge, because the engine was rated at a dull 140 bhp, drove through an automatic gearbox, and could just about haul the car from zero to sixty in ten seconds, with standing quarters in the 17-second range. Given that this was the "performance" option, the sluggishness of the smaller-engined cars cannot be contemplated with equanimity and certainly do not bare comparison with Mustangs of previous years.

In 1975, the Ghia grew opera windows and a vinyl half-roof. Add the crushed cranberry red velour interior which also came with the Silver Luxury Group in that year, and you

have a traveling boudoir on wheels – a far cry from anything that could decently and honestly be called a Mustang.

Worse still, in 1976 Ford also revived the Cobra name, but purely as a cosmetic package, though they did have the grace to exclude 4-cylinder models from the Cobra options. *Aficionados* of Carrol Shelby's magnificent originals (see Chapter 8) lay awake at night thinking of appropriate ends for Ford's marketing men; the general consensus was that lowering them inch by inch into boiling oil was probably too good for them. But Ford owned the rights to the Cobra name, as they did to the Ghia name, and no one could stop them.

ABOVE *The Cobra II was thus basically a trim option, which in 1976 comprised white and blue tape stripes, remote-control door mirrors, sports steering wheel and radial tyres among other goodies.*

In 1977 there was a tentative step back towards convertibles, in the form of the "T-roof" with its removable panels – but without the power to propel the car quickly, this was mainly useful if you liked a gentle breeze through your hair.

Finally, Ford introduced the King Cobra in 1978. This expensive option – $1,277 – was again primarily cosmetic, though it did include improved suspension and light-alloy wheels.

Of course, you can put a 351 engine into a Mustang II, and it is not too clear why Ford never officially did so; even the "cooking" version could have given some 50 percent more power than the 302, which would lift the power-to-weight ratio from 95 bhp/ton (the

V8 Mustang II weighed an alarming 3,290 lb) to over 140 bhp/ton. On the other hand, Ford may have decided that this would not be responsible, and it cannot be denied that a 60/40 front/rear weight distribution would not have done a lot for handling; and this is about what a 351 would have entailed.

In 1978, Ford built 192,410 Mustangs. In 1977, they had built 153,173; in 1976, 187,567; in 1975, 188,575; and in 1974, their best year. they had made 385,993, as already mentioned. It was clear that if the Mustang II was not a failure, it was not a success either and whilst it may have few fans today, it did serve to keep the "ponycar" tradition alive in Detroit during the seventies.

BELOW *The Mach I was also available as a T-top (picture) and with a V8 engine.*

T E C H N I C A L   S P E C I F I C A T I O N

MODEL	1974 Mustang
LENGTH	175 inches (4445 mm)
WIDTH	70.2 inches (1783 mm)
HEIGHT	50.3 inches (1278 mm)
KERB WEIGHT	2700 lb (1227 kg) approx
WHEELBASE	96.2 inches (2443 mm)
TRACK	Front: 55.6 inches (1412 mm) Rear: 55.8 inches (1417 mm)
WEIGHT	Distribution (front/rear): 59/41
ENGINE	Rated bhp (SAE gross) 88 Swept volume 140 cubic inches (2294 cc) Bore 3.78 inches (96 mm) Stroke 3.126 inches (79 4 mm) Compression ratio 8.4:1
PERFORMANCE	0–60 mph 15 seconds if you were lucky Standing Quarter Over 20 seconds Top speed Just over 100 mph

Note: Performance figures can vary very widely, according to the rear axle ratio chosen, the preparation of the car, weather conditions. and the mechanical sympathy (or otherwise) of the driver.

THE NEW GENERATION

After Mustang II, what next? Mustang III? No: just a reversion to the old, plain "Mustang" name.

The new 1979 Mustangs were 4.1 inches longer overall, at 179.1 inches; the extra length was used to give more interior space. The wheelbase increased by a slightly greater amount – 4.2 inches, from 96.2 inches to 100.4 inches – which made for a smoother ride. Width declined by 1.1 inches to 69.1 inches, while height increased by a surprising 1.6 inches to 51.9 inches – the tallest Mustang ever, though the lowest was 50.1 inches (1971-1973), so the variation was not all that great. The front track grew one inch (55.6 to 56.6 inches), while the rear track was increased by 1.2 inches. Best of all, the weight actually went *down* from the Mustang II: the heaviest cars had the 302 cid V8 and were catalogued with a weight of 3075 lb, a saving of well over 200 lb when compared with the previous model.

Washington was keen that the lessons of the energy crisis did not go unheeded by designers and leaders in Detroit, and hurriedly introduced CAFE (corporate average fuel economy) legislation. By penalizing companies whose fleet average fuel consumption exceeded the legal limits, Washinton effectively compelled Detroit to build lighter, thriftier and more aerodynamic cars. Ford duly obeyed and reduced the drag coefficient (C_d) to 0.44 for the fastback and 0.46 for the sedan. Although this was nothing remarkable by world standards (several manufacturers had already broken the 0.40 barrier), it was about 25 percent better than the Mustang II. Even with the same old 2.3 liter engine, performance was detectably better and fuel economy was also improved.

Unfortunately, the oil shortage soon became an oil glut and Washington no longer insisted quite so adamantly on observation of CAFE.

The wider track was complemented by new suspension – McPherson struts at the front, coil springs and a 4-link axle location at the rear – which did no harm whatsoever to the handling. Steering remained rack and pinion, and brakes were the same disc/drum combination that had been introduced on the Mustang II: an excellent combination, which there was no reason to change.

Nor was styling neglected. The fastback was introduced as a three-door or hatchback with quite pleasing styling, and although the two-door sedan was a bit generic, it was perfectly competent.

The net result was a car that could, with the right engine, be a very attractive package indeed. Unfortunately, finding the right engine was still problematical.

The basic engine was still the 88 bhp 2.3-liter all-metric four, making for about 69 bhp/ton (4-cylinder cars were catalogued at 2,861 lb), but during the 1979 model year there were no fewer than four other possibilities, some of them actually worse than the 88 bhp version.

Initially, the 2.8-liter German V6 remained an option, with its resounding 109 bhp and just over 80 bhp/ton. Then, half way through the model year, it was replaced by the old 200 cid straight-six, albeit now called a 3.3-liter engine as America began its struggle with metrication. Extraordinarily enough, though, this elderly mill was rated at a mere 85 bhp, actually *less* than the smaller, lighter in-line four!

The turbocharged version of the 2.3-liter four was also problematic. It looked great on

RIGHT *The '79 Cobra may not have pleased those who remembered Carroll Shelby, but it was a considerably better car than its immediate predecessors: roomier, yet lighter and with a lower drag coefficient (Cd), and with the option of either the 302 cid V8 or (as here) the turbo four.*

paper: 132 bhp from a power unit that weighed very little more than the unblown engine on which it was based, so that the power-to-weight ratio was almost identical to that of the V8. Unfortunately, though, it suffered from all the problems of first-generation turbos. Reliability was very poor, especially given the desultory maintenance which most American cars receive in their native land; low-end response was much weaker than the V8, because almost by definition a turbocharged engine becomes more efficient at higher engine speeds; and turbo lag was a serious problem and potentially dangerous. In the words of one driver of an early turbocharged Mustang (an Australian accountant, as it happens):

"You saw a place to overtake, so you put your foot down, and nothing happened. Just when you realized that you were not going to be able to overtake in time, and switched your foot to the brake, the turbocharger caught up with the engine and there was a big power surge. In effect, you were braking and accelerating at the same time, which could get pretty frightening."

Despite this, the turbo four was standard equipment on the Cobra Mustang, which also received Michelin 190/65R 390 TRX tires. These were an option on other Mustangs, and a highly desirable one – provided you did not mind being locked into exactly the same replacement tires, which were all that would fit onto the special 15.4-inch wheels with their 5.9-inch (150-mm) rims.

ABOVE AND OPPOSITE TOP *In 1979 Ford capitalized on the opportunity to serve as the official pace car by producing 11,000 Special Editions.*

The 302 cid/5.0-liter engine therefore remained the most desirable option, though with a 2-barrel carburetter and a modest 140 bhp rating, it was not exactly the basis for a road-burner. Then again, the power that it could supply was too much for the stock rear suspension: wheel hop and axle tramp were all too obvious if the driver wanted to try traditional American-style drag starts. Even so, it did break the 100 bhp/ton figure which is a convenient dividing line between powerful cars and the rest.

For the "collector" – the buyer who is always impressed by a "special edition", no matter how many are made or how manufactured the excuse for the "edition" may be – there was the Pace Car; in 1979, the

BELOW *The 302 cid –
now called a "5 liter" –
was the engine that most
people bought if they
could afford it.*

new Mustang was chosen as the pace car for the Indianapolis 500. The pace cars were fitted with hopped-up 302-cid (5-liter) engines, but the "replicas" (of which some 11,000 were built) were available with either the "cooking" 302 cid V8 or the turbo four.

The most interesting thing about the Pace Car, though, was probably the bodywork. It was a "T-top", that curious 1970s nod in the direction of a convertible, where panels on either side of a central roof "spine" could be removed while still maintaining almost all of the structural integrity of a sedan: structural integrity that translates into better rigidity, lighter weight, and better crash protection than a true convertible.

With the top (tops?) off, the Pace Car was inclined to be noisy, and anyone who was

willing to risk deafness by exploring the upper reaches of the performance range would find that it was significantly slower than the regular fastback; but it looked good, and it gave you the wind in your hair, and anyway it was mainly intended for tootling along at 55 mph, or maybe a little faster. The front air dam and rear spoiler were more for image than for effect, and the big, rear-facing air scoop on the hood was purely ornamental; it served no engineering function whatsoever.

All Pace Cars came with the same pewter and black bodywork, though the graphics (galloping ponies – again – and a great deal of text which began "OFFICIAL PACE CAR") were applied either by the dealer or by the buyer. Many buyers left the graphics off altogether; some installed just the ponies; but

BELOW AND OPPOSITE
For 1980, Ford downgraded the V8 from 5 liters and 140 bhp to 4.2 liters and 119 bhp; the only hope for the performance enthusiast was the turbo engine. Revised side graphics on these Cobras distinguish them from 1979 models.

WILL THE '83 GT CONVERTIBLE BE "WORTH SOMETHING?"

I n 1982 Ford reintroduced the Mustang GT and, in 1983, the Mustang convertible. It would have made sense for Ford to produce as many '83 Mustang GT convertibles as possible, but the only GTs available at the start of the year had solid tops or optional T roofs. The majority of convertibles were GLX models. A few GT convertibles were produced during the final weeks of the model year, more to promote the '84 Mustangs than to fill a niche in the '83 lineup.

In January 1987, Lauren Jonas Fix, national sales manager for Stainless Steel Brakes Corporation and a true performance Ford fan, began searching for a convertible daily driver. At Colonial Ford, in Buffalo, New York, she found this 200-mile '83 GT "demo" model with original exhaust and tires. Ford's local district office informed Lauren that her convertible had been displayed at the New York Auto Show to promote the '84 models. It had remained in a manager's garage until he was transferred to Detroit, then offered for sale. Lauren jumped at the chance.

The exact number of '83 GTs produced in Detroit by Cars and Concepts remains a question, but the cars featured power windows, leather boots and shifter knobs, tilt wheels, air conditioning, cruise control, Premium sound AM/FM cassette players, power tops, five-speed transmissions, and tinted windows. The engines were first-year 302-4Vs, and the Posi-traction 2.73:1 rearends turned TRX wheels and 220/55HR-390 tires.

Fortunately, Lauren Jonas Fix is aware of the uniqueness of her Mustang. Everything on the car, she claims, will be left in its original state. Because hobbyists already have begun to restore early '80s Mustangs, this particular group of '83 GTs might be considered collectible at this moment. In this case, the future is now.

very few seem to have felt that their car would be greatly enhanced by the full text of Ford's official *communiqué*. One strong argument against using the Pace Car graphics was that they were effectively an open invitation to any speed cop who was under quota that month . . .

In the first model year with the third-generation body, Ford made just under 370,000 Mustangs (the actual total was 369,936), which was a marked improvement over the previous year, when they had sold under 200,000 of the Mustang II. The question was, could they keep the sales up?

For the 1980 model year, changes were mostly slight, and mostly of no consequence – though tungsten-halogen headlights, a maintenance-free battery, and P-metric tires were all for the better, while on the engine front there was a mixture of good news and bad news. The good news was modest enough: the long-suffering straight-six gained a few horsepower, with 91 bhp in the manual-transmission cars and 95 bhp if you ordered the slush-box, and that even the base four managed to find 90 bhp in auto-transmission form. The bad news, though, was very bad indeed: the 5.0-liter V8 was reduced to 4.2 liters (by reducing the bore from 4 inches to 3.68 inches), and that its output was reduced to 119 bhp.

It is very hard to see why this happened. Perhaps Ford's marketing men had it in mind to promote the turbo four, without realizing that it was inherently a disaster area which would soon have to be dropped. Perhaps they were too worried about the skittishness of the rear end with the 140 bhp engine. Whatever the reasoning (if reason there was) it did nothing for the born-again Mustang's credibility. There was a new 5-speed manual overdrive option (though the V8 was available only as an automatic), but this was mostly of academic interest as there was not really enough engine available to drive it. There were the usual go-faster "styling cues" such as air dams, spoilers, and lots of black-out paint, but as so often in the history of the

LEFT *As they had done more than 15 years before, Ford tried to pitch the Mustang at the younger car buyer. Perhaps this was a good idea: with the base engine fitted to this '81 model, they were unlikely to go fast enough to get into serious trouble.*

MUSTANG'S SURVIVING FOREFATHER

DONALD PETERSON HAS BEEN ALONG FOR THE RIDE SINCE THE MUSTANG WAS BORN

They came from points all over the U.S., Canada and even Europe, Mustang fans old and young, to celebrate the 25th anniversary of the April 1964 introduction of Ford's famed ponycar. The place was Knotts Berry Farm in Buena Park, California, a suburb of Los Angeles. Each year, Knotts Berry Farm sponsors an all-Ford show featuring some of the finest creations to roll out of Dearborn. In 1989, the focus was naturally on the Mustang, and showgoers who came to honor the car weren't disappointed.

topline performer again. He's seen it all and still watches over the Mustang herd today.

For Petersen, the story began in 1949 when he joined Ford fresh out of Stanford's business school, where he got his MBA. Originally trained in mechanical engineering at the University of Washngton, he first tackled product programming analysis.

"The company did not then use the title 'product planning,'" remembers Petersen. "In my early years, I helped set up the first systems that

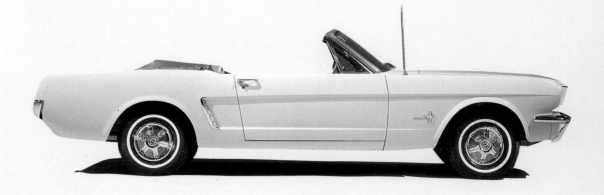

If anyone deserved to sit at the head of the table at the Mustang's 25th birthday celebration it was Petersen. Henry Ford II, Lee Iacocca, Donald Frey, Joe Oros, Gene Bordinat all departed in various directions; design chief Bordinat passing away August 11, 1987, followed by Henry Ford II six weeks later. Donald Petersen remains, serving as Ford president since 1980 after working his way up the ladder in much the same fashion Iacocca did 20 years ago. Along the way, he has witnessed firsthand the Mustang's entire history, from a free-thinker's dream, to mass-market marvel, to musclebound performance car, to scaled-down econo-cruiser, to resized and revived sportster, to

built a bridge between Ford division and engineering and styling. Prior to that, engineering and manufacturing would design and build the vehicle independently, and then the sales people were handed the product, with no creative input from division management". He would stay in this role until late 1963, when he moved to marketing to arrange similar links.

It was through these links that the Mustang came to be. A knowledge of what was missing in the model line and what the public was waiting for, combined with an awareness of what was and wasn't selling out in the marketplace helped foster the ponycar ideal, an ideal that originated from a handful of minds, not just one. According to Petersen, transforming the Thunderbird from two-seater to four in 1958 created a gap in the model line as far as the sporty-minded customer was concerned. But a two-seater would never sell enough copies, a conclusion all involved came to at an early date, even though the Mustang I "prototype" (which was a two-seater) was built and openly publicized in 1962.

It was product planning manager Donald Frey who helped define the niche. "Donald kept hounding me about a sports car", Petersen said. "Initially, he was pushing for a Corvette fighter, the type of car we had gone away from when we dropped the little 'Bird. Concurrently, we were kind of interested in a very successful 2+2 coming out of Europe, the Renault Dauphine, which was selling rather well. We were also watching the (Corvair) Monza. And so (Frey) and I were sufficiently positive about the market for a new car, and set up a special project with Hal Sperlich as the manager under me".

Frey, Petersen and division general manager Lee Iacocca, then came to the conclusion in spring 1962 that a competitively priced 2+2 was the answer. Much of the rest seems an awful lot like odd luck, contrary to the commonly told tale of precise market research and product analysis. But in fact, the Mustang was more a result of sound on-the-spot decision making and decisiveness, moves made possible through the communications link Petersen mentioned. Though timing in the marketplace had something to do with the Mustang's overwhelming sales success, so too did the fact that Iacocca and crew saw an opportunity and went for it relatively without a flinch.

So it was once the decision was made on a "competitively priced 2+2", it became the stylists turn to make contributions. And in June 1962, Joe Oros made his. According to Petersen, "one day Joe came walking down the hall with a sketch under his arm on a 40-by-60-inch board. Iacocca, Sperlich, Frey, Gene Bordinat, myself and others were present, and when Joe showed us the sketch, it just clicked, and that was the car that became the Mustang. Once we had a full-sized clay model that

clinched it. We were able then to have agreement – to let her rip"!

Optimism among the planners quickly grew, from initial proposals of 150,000 units a year to final preparations for sales in excess of 300,000, all this developing off what Petersen recalls as very little market research. "I remember spending a lot of time with Sperlich, contemplating what was happening with the market. I remember discussing the 2+2 cars that existed and what was happening to the Corvair". Contemplation and discussion – other than that, the rest was pure guts.

Of course, not all decisions went so well. Not everyone agreed with the 1967 restyle and decreasing sales echoed that disagreement. In response, Petersen pointed out that "the original Mustang was a smash hit, but one criticism people levelled at it was that it wasn't muscular enough. So there was great pressure almost from the very start for a bolder, more powerful-looking design". As a result, the Mustang started gaining weight, both to make room for larger engines and to take on a more "powerful look". Many, including Donald Frey, still think the restyle was a bad move. "It was a mistake" claimed Frey. "I regret being a party to it. I had bosses too, and I didn't like it but agreed anyway".

Mistake or not, Petersen wasn't so sure. "During those years there were two paths to the Mustang's evolution. One path was formed from this great desire to build more muscle into the car, which culminated in the extremes of the Boss 429. And the other path (involved) the very high-volume (potential) of economical six-cylinder Mustangs we sold at very attractive prices". Unfortunately, the two didn't mix well, but that's some of what product planning is about.

Petersen moved from marketing to product planning in 1967, then became head of truck operations in 1971, and finally was made Ford Motor Company president in March 1980. Though far removed, he's never lost his feeling for what happened 25 years ago, and was it any wonder he personally picked a '65 Mustang convertible as winner of the "best of show" award at the Knotts Berry Farm show?

Mustang, they had lovers of fast cars grinding their teeth: the 1980 models were slugs in sprinters' clothing. As a result production fell to 271,322 cars.

Nor was 1981 much better. The turbo was deleted early in the year: bad news for techno-freaks, but good news for anyone who might actually have been tempted to buy one. Options included a limited slip differential, power windows, and a T-roof (on both body styles, at a stiff $916), but the overall reaction of most enthusiasts was, "So what?"

There was an attempt at a serious go-faster Mustang, though: the McLaren Mustang. Based on the ill-starred Turbo, this was a Mustang that was extensively "breathed upon" by the well-known McLaren racing concern, with lots of hand-finishing and clever stuff. The trouble was that it listed for about $25,000; and although it was a remarkably sweet-handling car which could be thrown around with considerable *elan*, it was arguably too far ahead of its time.

Buyers of American "performance" cars are traditionally obsessed with the time for the standing quarter mile: cornering, braking, and other considerations are distinctly secondary. In the case of the McLaren Mustang, the time for the standing quarter mile was a modest 17 seconds or so; and although the handling and everything else were very good, and would probably have ensured the sale of the car if it had come from some little-known European manufacturer, it was not a great success.

In the 1982 model year, though, Ford began to turn the corner and to re-establish the Mustang as a car that one might actually want to buy for fun, instead of for transport. When they did so, they probably did not suspect that their re-vamp of the rather tired and less than entirely successful third-generation Mustang would see them into the last decade of the twentieth century – but then, they never really knew what hit them when they introduced the original Mustang.

T E C H N I C A L S P E C I F I C A T I O N	
MODEL	1979 Cobra Mustang
LENGTH	179.1 inches (4549 mm)
WIDTH	69.1 inches (1755 mm)
HEIGHT	51.9 inches (1318 mm)
KERB WEIGHT	2900 lb (1318 kg) approx.
WHEELBASE	100.4 inches (2550 mm)
TRACK	Front: 56.6 inches (1438 mm) Rear: 57 inches (1448 mm)
WEIGHT	Distribution (front/rear): 57/43
ENGINE	Rated bhp (SAE gross) 132 Swept volume 140 cubic inches (2294 cc) Bore 3.781 inches (96 mm) Stroke 3.126 inches (79.4 mm) Compression ratio 9.0:1
PERFORMANCE	0–60 mph Under 10 seconds Standing Quarter Around 15 seconds Top speed Over 120 mph

Note: Performance figures can vary very widely, according to the rear axle ratio chosen, the preparation of the car, weather conditions, and the mechanical sympathy (or otherwise) of the driver.

BELOW *The turbo – here seen in its 1980 guise – suffered from all the defects of first-generation turbos, but when it was going, it went rather well.*

RETURN TO GLORY

T he most immediately obvious improvement in the 1982 Mustang line-up was the re-introduction of the 5-liter engine, this time as the "HO" (High Output), with a very welcome 157 bhp: there were a number of interior improvements, such as a duplex timing chain, a slightly higher-lift cam, and general beefing up. If you bought the 5-liter, you had to have a manual gearbox (as distinct from the 4.2-liter which was only available with a slush-box), and you had to have the limited slip differential, power brakes, power steering, and a "handling package" of suspension improvements. Cast alloy wheels were standard.

The 5-liter was available for any Mustang, though it was standard (along with a large number of other options) on the GT. The only catch was the bottom line: a T-top GT would cost you $9,500, and it was possible to spend $10,000 on a Mustang without trying too hard; almost four times as much as the original base car in 1964, in the space of less than 20 years.

For 1983, the rated horsepower of the HO rose to 175, still in a vehicle that weighed under 3,100 lb: a power-to-weight ratio of better than 125 bhp/ton, achieved largely with the help of a 4-barrel Holley 600 cfm carburetter on a light-alloy manifold. Wider, lower-profile tires helped to keep the show on the road: 205/70HT x 14 instead of 185/75R x 14 became standard on all GT models.

Not only that, there were also two new engine options. One was a resurrected version of the 2.3-liter Turbo, enormously improved in reliability *and* uprated to 145 bhp for a power-to-weight ratio of better than 110 bhp/ton. The other was an all-new 2.8-liter

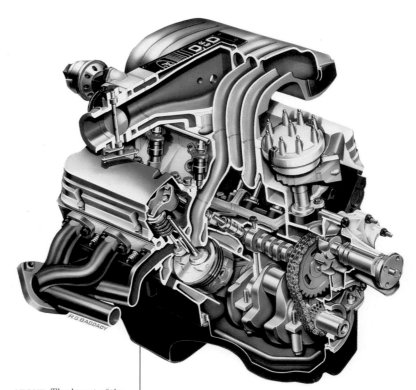

ABOVE *The heart of the matter: the seemingly immortal 302 cid (5 liter) engine, here in its 1987 HO (High Output) incarnation which delivered a very comfortable 225 bhp SAE net – probably well over 250 bhp SAE gross.*

V6, with alloy heads and a rated 112 bhp for just over 85 bhp/ton: not a powerful engine, perhaps, but one that delivered quite adequate power in a smooth, reliable form and was arguably the best choice for the driver who was not in love with raw power

Still further to gladden the enthusiast's heart, the Ford Mustang convertible finally reappeared after a 10-year absence. It had the classic disadvantages of convertibles – dubious weatherproofing (though the T-roof was not always watertight, either), reduced space in the rear, extra weight, less rigidity, increased wind noise – but hey, who cared? All convertibles are like that, and besides, this was what Mustangs were supposed to be about: FUN, in capital letters.

A 5-liter GT convertible would have set you back $13,500 in 1983, but it was a real car, with a real 5-speed manual gearbox as standard and all kinds of other goodies, including a traditionally massive list of options, though the ones you really needed were thankfully included in the price. It even had a power roof, with a glass rear window – a proper *American* convertible, brought up to date.

After a very long period in the doldrums, the Mustang was really beginning to look good again; but amazingly, total production in 1983 was a miserable 120,873. Of those, just over a quarter (33,201) were sedans; just under a fifth (23,438) were convertibles; and the remaining 64,234 cars were three-door hatchbacks, rather over one-half of total production. Unless sales went up, it looked as though the days of the Mustang – *any* Mustang – might be numbered.

BELOW *Alloy wheels, lots of lights, and a black bumper/rubbing strip: this 1982 5-liter looked fast and actually was fast. Better still, it was not just a straight-line special: it handled and cornered much better than many of its contemporaries.*

LEFT *Red on red: an 83 convertible with the 5-liter engine. If you wanted ultimate performance, you probably wouldn't choose the convertible, but if you wanted the most enjoyable Mustang on the road, you would be sorely tempted.*

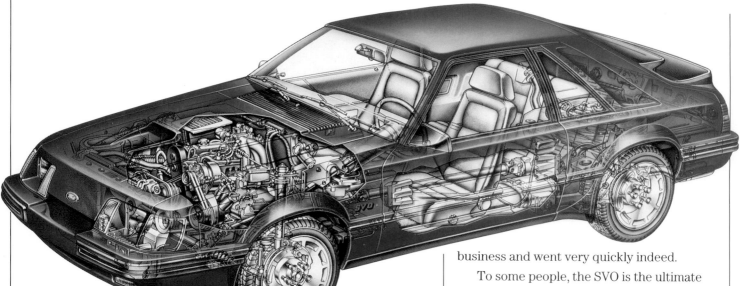

Nevertheless, things were beginning to look good for the enthusiast; now was the winter of our discontent made glorious spring. And, in fact, the suspension was the next thing that Ford overhauled. In 1984, Quadra-Shock rear suspension appeared, offering improved control of the sometimes excessively live rear axle – though admittedly, it only appeared on one vehicle in the line-up, the SVO (see below). At last, though, there was a chance to get most of the power on the road, and there was also a return to the days of the bewildering engine options. According to choice, you got a straight four, a V6, or a V8.

At the bottom of the heap, there was the same old reliable 88-bhp 2.3-liter engine; but it was also available in 145 bhp Turbo GT form (as in 1983) and in a limited-edition 175-bhp variant which appeared in the middle of the model year.

The 175 bhp motor, running a maximum 14 lb boost and equipped with an intercooler and electronic fuel injection, was installed in the Mustang SVO – for "Special Vehicle Operations", the performance division of FoMoCo. There were Koni adjustable shockers on the front end, four-wheel discs, Quadra-Shocks, bucket seats with adjustable lumbar support, leather steering wheel, and 16 x 7 inch light-alloy wheels. With a biplane rear spoiler, functioning hood scoop, and a uniquely styled grille, the SVO looked the

ABOVE *The Good Stuff: the reborn turbo four in the 1984 SVO. If you can face the rigors of turbo maintenance, this is arguably one of the great Mustangs. The very anthithesis of a straight-line special, this is a car to be driven at high speeds on winding roads.*

business and went very quickly indeed.

To some people, the SVO is the ultimate third-generation Mustang. It has as much power as the V8, in a lighter, better-balanced, better-handling package. But, as already noted, that is not necessarily what plays in Peoria. The V8 had considerably more low-end urge, which translated directly into what American motoring writers call "visceral excitement" and Europeans call "brute power". For the fast driver, the SVO is and will probably remain the ultimate production Mustang; but a comparatively small number of

Mustang buyers are interested in the finer points of driving. Their interests are raw acceleration, speed on the straight, cruising comfort, and looks.

Also, the price of the SVO was $15,585 at the time of its introduction. Given that the 5-liter GT was still (just) under $10,000, and given the well-deserved reputation that turbo cars have for needing considerably more careful maintenance than a big ol' V8, it is perhaps easy to see why the SVO did not do better. Besides, people have a distressing tendency to believe that if you want a good car, you have to buy a European import (and if you want a reliable car, it has to be a Japanese import). As a result, Americans sometimes underrate their own best cars.

To return to the engine options, though, the 3.8-liter V6 was still available, this time with fuel injection to boost the power to 120 bhp, which meant a power-to-weight ratio comfortably in excess of 90 bhp/ton. Then, the 5-liter V8 was available in two forms. With the manual gearbox, it still had the 600 cfm Holley and 175 bhp, but if you opted for the (4-speed) automatic, you got electronic fuel injection which gave, somewhat unexpectedly, a *lower* power rating of 165 bhp.

What was more, 1984 marked the 20th anniversary of the Mustang; and they did not hesitate to capitalize on this. Production figures were not up very much, with well under 150,000 Mustangs built, but 5,260 of these were 20th Anniversary Specials: 350 Turbo GTs; 3,333 5.0L GTs; 104 Convertible Turbo GTs; 120 Convertible 5.0L GTs; plus 15 "VIP" convertibles and 245 vehicles from Ford of Canada. As usual, this was a cosmetic package with no performance pretensions, though (as can be seen) only top-of-the-line cars were available as Anniversary specials.

All anniversary models were painted white with red interiors, and came with two 20th Anniversary dash panel badges. The first came with the car, and the second was sent on a few months later and had the owner's name engraved on it – a nice touch, though some owners forgot (or did not bother) to have the second badge installed. To those Mustang-lovers whose appreciation of cars is more akin

OVERLEAF The fixed–head Mustangs are not quite so classic as the drop–heads, and the line between "fastback" and "hardtop" is more blurred than it was; in fact, the "fastback" is now a "hatchback".

BELOW Which would you rather have? The original, or the 20th Anniversary Convertible? The newer car would be smoother, more economical, better-handling, and probably faster, so if you want an easy life, there's no question. But if you were actually given the choice....

to philately than to engineering, the presence or absence of these plaques makes an enormous difference to the value of the car.

As an aside, during this model year Ford took over the production of the convertibles from Cars & Concepts, the outside contractor who had hitherto been responsible for the softtops; but again, this is of interest more to lovers of minutiae than to lovers of motor cars.

For 1985, production continued to climb: 156,514 Mustangs were made, the vast majority of them hatchbacks (84,623), and less than ten per cent of them convertibles (15,110). The front end treatment changed to a rather ugly and generic slope, and the ordinary or garden-variety Mustangs were much the same as the previous year; but at the top end of the model range, there was a wonderful combination of more power *and* better handling.

The 5-liter was reworked to give no less than 210 bhp, via a threefold line of attack. The most obvious, as soon as you opened the hood, was the new exhaust system: a stainless-steel dual system, instead of the old cast-iron manifold. This alone was worth a good deal of power. Inside, the camshaft was reprofiled and equipped with roller cam-followers, which is another fine traditional way to get more power. And third, a new approach was tried, a different accessory drive system which ran the alternator, power steering pump, and air conditioner (where fitted) at half engine speed except at idle. This was most significant at the top end of the power band, because much of the power that is supplied to these accessories is "thrown away" at high engine speeds, sapping engine power without any benefit.

This last trick is particularly significant, as it clearly demonstrates the new thinking of motor manufacturers, especially American motor manufacturers, and illustrates why modern cars are vastly more fuel-efficient than their predecessors, and often faster as well. The traditional approach was simply *more power*. If this meant more weight, so be it; the answer was more power again . . . And if accessories such as alternators or power steering pumps or air conditioners sapped power from the engine; why, just build a bigger engine!

This way of building fast cars dated back to the earliest days, with the Itala, the 200 HP Mercedes, the Lion Peugeot, and others; and of course it had been seen in the big *Kompressor* Mercedes of the 1920s and 1930s, and their contemporaries the big Bentleys, notably the 8-liter. The only problem with such an approach is that a big, heavy car is inevitably less nimble and responsive than a small, light one; which is why power-to-weight ratios are only a part of the story.

There had, however, been a long-standing alternative European tradition, followed only by a few makers, of building much lighter cars, which required less brute power to drive them and were much easier to "chuck around". The classical examples are probably the Bugattis

BELOW *The '87s came with a bewildering variety of wheels – but they were almost all cosmetically quite attractive, though obviously light-alloy was the way to go if you could afford it.*

of the 1920s and 1930s, and indeed it was Ettore Bugatti who said, "This M'sieur Bentley, he builds the fastest trucks in the world".

Other adherents of light, fast cars included Aston Martin (at least before the war, though even a DB2 is still a surprisingly light motor car), BMW (with the 327 and 328 series), Bristol, Porsche, and various Italians, but until the 1970s and 1980s, this was not a mainstream approach. The fact that Ford was now beginning to pay attention to such finicky questions as aerodynamics (genuine, not cosmetic – most "streamlining" of American cars before that time was totally ineffective) and conserving engine power was a clear indication that the mainstream was beginning to change direction.

And speaking of light, fast cars, the Turbo was also uprated, though not quite to the same extent as the V8: you got 205 bhp for

your $14,806, the extra power coming mostly from a further one-pound of turbo boost, combined with a new inlet manifold, a hotter camshaft, an easier-breathing exhaust, and bigger fuel injection nozzles. With a catalog weight (unless you added too many accessories) of under 3,000 lb, this meant well over 150 bhp/ton, or considerably better than twice the power to weight ratio of the unblown base engine.

The steering ratio of the SVO was 14.7:1 (about twice as quick as the original Mustang), the ride was stiffened yet again, and stabilizer bar bushings were Teflon-lined.

All this, together with Goodyear Eagles in place of the old NCT tires, made for a very remarkable package in which the power-to-weight ratio and the front/rear balance were both much better than the V8. To make the car still more desirable, the engine mounting was revised so that passengers were better isolated from the vibration of the big four; this made the new SVO a rather more pleasant vehicle to drive for long distances.

As before, though, the SVO was a car that was better suited to European conditions than to American ones, where low speed limits, generally straight roads, and a more casual attitude towards lane discipline meant that a quick, nimble car was nothing like as much fun as it might be in, say, England or Italy. It is worth making a comparison with Germany, where the very high speeds on the *autobahns* are made possible by two things. One is that entrances and exits are far less frequent than on most American "freeways", and the other is that overtaking "on the inside" (ie the nearside or left) is *verboten*. Try it, and if you're lucky, you'll get a ticket. If you are unlucky, you'll kill yourself.

This European orientation is one of the reasons why the V8 remained the most popular engine. Other reasons included the price of the turbo SVO (the V8 was about $4,000 cheaper), the admitted superiority of the V8 in a drag race, and the fact that the V8 is significantly easier to maintain. The 1985 model year also saw the Quadra-Shock rear axle adopted as standard on the GT V8s, together with a bigger stabilizer bar and

FAR RIGHT *Somehow, the slight dip in the hatch back of the "fastback" seems to compromise its lines: the old, straight lines of the earlier muscle cars are cleaner and more decisive.*

BELOW *The brake–cooling scoops at both front and rear are the most obvious distinguishing marks between this 1987 5.0L GT Convertible and the four-cylinder version. From a purely stylistic point of view, the "four" is arguably more elegant.*

P225/60VR-15 unidirectional tires, the Goodyear Eagle Gatorbacks. These new tires were mounted on 7-inch rims, but such were the changes in tire technology that they could not fairly be compared with the taller, narrower, less sticky tires fitted to the same size rims on, say, the Boss 429. Also, the wheels on the 1985 GTs were light alloy, not chrome steel; and when you are dealing with fast, powerful cars, any reduction in unsprung weight is extremely desirable.

Another improvement was a reduction in the throw of the T-5 (manual 5-speed) transmission, which made gear shifting quicker and more enjoyable. At last, for the first time since 1964, it seemed that Ford was getting its act together on the sporting front.

Of course, if you wanted one of the lesser Mustangs, they would cheerfully sell you one: the automatic V8 was still rated at 165 bhp, and the other options were still the 3.8-liter V6 (120 bhp) and the 88-bhp 2.3-liter.

For 1986, changes were minimal, though the big V8 actually lost 10 bhp when it switched over to sequential port fuel injection – a remarkable accomplishment, when you consider that just about every other manufacturer in the world got *more* power by using fuel injection. In all fairness, FoMoCo was hobbled by US emission requirements, but it still seems that they could have done better. This downrating had the interesting effect, though, that the turbo SVO (which remained at 205 bhp) was both more powerful than the V8 *and lighter* – well over 100 lb lighter. Although the V8 had it all in a drag race, for high-speed performance, the SVO was the winner!

For 1987, the classic SVO was dropped, and indeed the engine line-up was considerably reduced: the only choice was between the same old 88 bhp base engine, and the 5-liter V8, now uprated to no less than 225

bhp by means of redesigned heads (allegedly derived from those used on Ford trucks – shades of "This M'sieur Bentley . . .") and bigger throttle bodies. With that much power, and an impressive 300 lb/ft of maximum torque, the Mustang was now a "muscle car" in the style of the late 1980s.

The front-end styling was also much improved. It still bore a strong resemblance to other Fords, and was in that sense somewhat "generic", but it was handled with very much more assurance. The GTs acquired a "ground effect" skirt or air dam at the front, which wrapped all the way around to the rear and gave the car a closer-to-the-ground look. It could be awkward on steeply-angled driveways, and it was unlikely ever to be significant at the speeds production cars could be driven, but it actually was functional if you decided to use the full power of the V8 and to travel at velocities in excess of twice the legal speed limit, the well-known 55 mph joke.

If you did so, though, you would only be able to work out your speed by reference to the tachometer, because in their (rather elegantly) restyled dashboards, Mustangs still sported the other great American motoring joke, the 85 mph speedometer.

The logic of the 85 mph speedo seems to have been that 85 mph was 30 mph faster than the national speed limit; no-one could possibly have any excuse for going faster than 85 mph; and besides, if you didn't tell people how fast they were going, (a) they wouldn't be tempted to try to find out how fast they could go, and (b) they couldn't argue with the cops if they were nicked for traveling at more than 85 mph. This could be significant: the last time I was nicked for speeding in the United States, the cop tried to tell me I was exceeding 100 mph and that he could haul me off to jail. If I had been doing 95 in a 1987 Mustang, how could I have argued?

If you did decide to go illegally quickly, though, you would find that all kinds of good things from the now-defunct SVO would make it easier for you to do so: increased wheel

travel, alignment aimed at responsiveness rather than a "boulevard ride", a bigger stabilizer bar, bigger front discs (10.9 inches – though you still had 9-inch drums on the back), new light-alloy wheels, and more. You would also travel in greater comfort, thanks to admirably adjustable seats with power lumbar support and variable under-thigh support.

And that, at the time of writing, was about it. Model changes for 1988 and 1989 were minimal, though the speedometer was replaced with a more realistic 140 mph model on the 5-liter Mustangs in 1989, and in 1990 the driver's side grew an air bag. For the ordinary Mustang buyer, the most significant change probably took place for the 1991 model year, when the underpowered 2.3-liter four was uprated to 105 bhp by means of a twin-plug head and a 9.5:1 compression ratio. In the same year, the wheels on the go-faster models were changed from 15 inches to 16 inches, reflecting the ever-diminishing section of tires, while the 4-cylinder cars stayed with 14-inch wheels.

The sedan weighed an admirably modest 2,759 lb, so even with the base engine you could look forward to just over 85 bhp/ton – a very comfortable figure for every day driving, though scarcely sporting – while the convertible was rather over 200 lb heavier. Better still, the drag coefficient was down to 0.40 for the sedan, 0.38 for the regular hatchback, and 0.36 for the GT. This of course translates into quieter, faster, more relaxed high-speed cruising, a better top speed, and better fuel economy; or at least, into the potential for improvement in each of these areas, though there are inevitably trade-offs. For example, if you actually use that high-speed cruising ability, it will not do your fuel economy much good!

In other words, the Mustang was just about back where it started: all things to all men. Production figures for both 1988 and 1989 broke the 200,000 barrier, making the Mustang "the car that wouldn't die", somewhat to the puzzlement of its makers, but to the delight of its buyers. It was available

as a good-looking, reasonably-sized, *fun* motor car, with a choice of a comfortably quick base engine or a distinctly sporting go-faster engine – a motor which would, under the right conditions, take the needle all the way to the end of the 140 mph speedometer.

Of course, the new Mustangs are quieter, smoother, faster, and offer better handling than the old ones. Most of us, if we do not get a chance to drive "classic" cars, tend to look at the past through rose-tinted spectacles. The brutal truth is that old cars are mostly slow, thirsty, under-braked, and much more

ABOVE *One of the most interesting things about this picture is its photographic quality. After years of rather stolid, "all-in" pictures they began to use dramatic lines and compositions – much more exciting to look at!*

inclined to depart from the paths of righteousness when pressed too hard around a corner. Unless they were very expensive when they were new, they are also inclined to be noisy, and one of the most noticeable things when you get into the average old car is the small windows, which create a cramped or even claustrophobic atmosphere. An old Mustang – even a "classic" early '65, or a Boss – exhibits all these faults.

On the other hand, older cars are frequently endowed with something that newer cars lack; an indefinable something that we call character. In part, "character" is a result of defects: how often have you heard someone say of their beloved old car, "Ah, well, that's all a part of the character". Usually, they are talking about indifferent brakes (have you ever driven an old Daimler?), or inadequate heating (I have owned Triumph TR2, TR3 and TR4, and the only heat worth bothering with comes direct from the engine), or lousy windshield wipers (remember the old Ford vacuum-operated ones?), or poor weather sealing (try even a *new* Corvette in the rain) – all palpable defects. But what they mean is that despite its faults, and indeed in some ways because of them, their car has a personality of its own. Dismissively, they will call a new car an "appliance": like a refrigerator, or a kitchen stove, it is something that you buy to use, and it is hard to get excited about it.

RIGHT *This 1990 Special Edition has lines which are, for my money, among the best ever found on a Mustang convertible.*

BELOW *The "then and now" theme is always intriguing. This is a 1989 Special Convertible beside one of its ancestors.*

TECHNICAL SPECIFICATION

MODEL	1987 Mustang 5-liter
LENGTH	179.1 inches (4549 mm)
WIDTH	69.1 inches (1755 mm)
HEIGHT	51.9 inches (1318 mm)
KERB WEIGHT	3075 lb (1398 kg) approx.
WHEELBASE	100.4 inches (2550 mm)
TRACK	Front: 56.6 inches (1438 mm) Rear: 57 inches (1448 mm)
WEIGHT	Distribution (front/rear): 59/41
ENGINE	Rated bhp (SAE gross) 225 Swept volume 302 cubic inches (4949 cc) Bore 4 inches (101.6 mm) Stroke 3 inches (76.2 mm) Compression ratio 8.4:1
PERFORMANCE	0–60 mph Under 7 seconds Standing Quarter Around 14 seconds Top speed Around 140 mph

Note: Performance figures can vary very widely, according to the rear axle ratio chosen, the preparation of the car, weather conditions, and the mechanical sympathy (or otherwise) of the driver.

Where this "personality" comes from is hard to say. In part, it is the personality of the designer; in part, it is the accumulation of the personalities of the owner or owners of the car, which seem to impress themselves in some mysterious way into the very metal of the machine. In part, it is even the personality of an era: the massive, silent limousines of the 1930s, the gaudy monsters of the self-confident fifties, the do-your-own-thing philosophy of the sixties.

"Personality", or "character", may manifest itself either in looks, or in sound, or in performance, or in a score of other ways which are easier to appreciate than to describe. In the next chapter, we shall look at the ultimate "character" Mustangs: the Shelbys.

CARROLL SHELBY AND THE MUSTANG

Mustangs – especially the first series – always looked fast. Some even were fast. But if you want a seriously fast Mustang, a Mustang with the ultimate in character, style and presence, the word is, of course, Shelby.

Even a quarter of a century after the first Shelby GT350 Mustangs appeared, they were still regarded by many as the most desirable Mustangs ever made. The main reason for this

BELOW *The GT350 was one of the few Mustangs that really cried out to be "yumped". It was at home as a rally car, or as a racer – a very fine combination.*

is that the earliest Shelby Mustangs were out-and-out, no-compromise street racers; and in fact, with some of them, the "street" part of "street racer" takes a very secondary place.

The philosophy was simple. On Ford's side, they wanted a car which actually delivered all that a Mustang promised – and more. It is doubtful whether more than a handful of the gentlemen from Dearborn were genuinely interested in a racing program, but even the

most obdurate bean-counter could see that a really quick Mustang would win races (and headlines) and create a much-needed strong identity for the new car.

On Carroll Shelby's side, there was an opportunity that few of us could resist: the chance to take a car from a major manufacturer, and "show them how it should be done" from an enthusiast's point of view. Of course, an enthusiast's view of "how it should be done" is a very different proposition from a manufacturer's. In a production car, there are things like reliability, and economy, and driving comfort to consider; in an enthusiast's car, the most important thing is to go as quickly as possible, and other things can be subordinated to that.

Unlike most of us, though, Carroll Shelby knew what he was doing. For every enthusiast who has successfully re-ground combustion chambers with a power drill, or rebuilt an engine with a hotter cam and double (or triple) valve springs, there must be ten who actually *reduce* power (along with reliability) by their "go-faster" modifications. And as for the "boy racer" tricks such as reversing rims

ABOVE *The GT500, introduced in 1967, outsold its sibling by a ratio of two-to-one.*

BELOW *In the mid-to-late 1960s, Shelby Mustangs were serious competition cars: people actually bought them with the intention of racing.*

(for a wider track – and twice the chance of pulling the studs out of the wheel); well, suffice it to say that Shelby either did things properly, or left well enough alone. He also had a literal track record, with the traditionally hairy Shelby Cobra, a spectacularly quick piece of machinery which, like the Mustang, was powered by a big lump of American iron.

LEFT *After heart trouble cut short a brief but successful racing career, Shelby turned eventually to car designing, masterminding first the AC Cobra sports car then the highly prized Shelby Mustangs.*

The net result was a Mustang which was not intended for a daily commute to work. The clutch was stiff, and inclined to be an "on-off" affair. The brakes required (if anything) even more effort from the driver, because there was no power assistance; and without power assistance, the quick steering made for very heavy parking. The car was also damnably noisy: music to the ears of an enthusiast (at least at first), but less than endearing to the ears of the old lady next door and distinctly wearing on a long run. A long drive in a Shelby GT350, especially a GT350R (the racing variant) can be almost as tiring as making the same journey on a powerful sports motorcycle.

What did Mr Shelby do, then, to make the Mustang into a genuine, fire-breathing enthusiast's car? Well, how does this sound:

Start with a 1965 Wimbledon white Mustang, complete with the 289 cid engine rated at a base 271 bhp, and equipped with a 4-speed manual gearbox and Detroit Locker limited slip differential; a good place to start.

Now, throw away the old manifold and Autolite carburetter: install a high-rise intake and a 700 cfm Holley. This gets the fuel into the cylinders faster, more smoothly, and in greater quantities. To make sure that it gets out again after it has been burnt, remove the cast-iron exhaust manifolds and replace them with proper steel headers – the Tri-Y design – then replace the stock mufflers with straight-through glass-pack mufflers which exit just in front of the rear wheels. In this context, incidentally, the American term "mufflers" is considerably more accurate than the English term "silencer"; the roar of the engine might be slightly muffled, but it is certainly not completely silenced.

To help keep the brute cool, replace the stock oil pan (sump) with a cast light alloy version with more capacity and considerably better heat transfer abilities; it also looks better, which is not irrelevant. On the top end, add cast light alloy valve covers: a more modest gain in heat transfer here, but another considerable gain in looks.

All right: the engine is now delivering about 10 percent more power (306 bhp instead of 271 bhp). To keep track of the power, stick in a rev counter: peak power is at 6,000 rpm, but in case of necessity you can rev to 7,000 rpm, so make it an 8,000 rpm unit. Also add an oil pressure gauge. The two new "clocks" look a trifle incongruous in their special dash-top pod, on the driver's right above the stock Mustang instrumentation, but they are reasonably visible.

Now try to get the power on the road: begin with the suspension. Lower the upper control arm mounting points; stick in a *big* (one-inch) front stabilizer bar. At the back, put in over-the-axle traction bars in an attempt to control wheel hop and axle tramp when you floor the accelerator. Put rebound cables on the axle housing, and while you are at it, put a safety loop on the drive shaft. Oh, yes; and Koni shocks all round.

Improved suspension is inseparable from improved steering, so brace the front end properly: install a bigger, heavier brace between the firewall and the two shock towers (the "Export Brace" – maybe foreigners are less tolerant of hinge-in-the-middle handling?) and put a big transverse bar across from one side of the engine bay to the other: a "Monte Carlo" bar. This almost-triangulated reinforcement of the big engine bay removes the inclination of the front end to twist or "lozenge" during hard cornering. Now that you have a rigid front end, you can install special Pitman and idler arms for more precise steering. It still isn't rack and pinion, but it's a vast improvement over the stock steering arrangement.

The next thing to consider – and it is something that is all too easy to forget – is the brakes. This is something that even Ettore Bugatti neglected: as he once said imperiously to a customer, "I build my cars to go, not to stop!" The *maestro*'s comments notwithstanding, dinky little drums are not the way to go, so try discs on the front and

bigger drums (10 x 2½) on the back. You don't need power assistance: this is a no-compromise sports car, remember? You do, however, need legs like a Sumo wrestler.

You're winning: you have a more powerful, stronger, better-handling Mustang, which also stops. What do you do next?

Add some lightness, and improve the weight distribution. To "add lightness", replace the stock steel hood with one made of glass-reinforced plastic. While you're having a new hood made, you might as well have a functional air scoop: powerful engines like to have lots of cold air to breathe. Then, to improve the weight distribution (because the car is a bit nose-heavy), relocate the battery to the trunk.

You have to drive the thing, so you might as well be safe and comfortable. Put in big, wide competition seat belts (which are also more comfortable than street-type belts), and replace the plastic steering wheel with a grippier, more pleasant-feeling wood-rim version. You are not likely to want to carry rear-seat passengers, so rip out the rear seats and install a lighter, neater GRP shelf instead; this also makes a good place to put the spare wheel, as well as adding more lightness.

If you still have enough money left, finish the package off with Cragar mag-alloy wheels. You have now built yourself a very good approximation to a 1965 Shelby Mustang; assuming, that is, that you have used all the right bits. You can run standing quarters in the 14s, and zero-to-sixty times in the sixes.

If you are the Ford Motor Company, you also want it to be good and obvious that this is (a) a Mustang, and (b) a very special Mustang. You therefore make a number of cosmetic modifications, such as removing all Mustang emblems except the ones on the gas cap and the radiator, and you move the one on the radiator to the extreme left. You add side stripes that say "GT350", and if you want to get *really* dramatic you also add the front-to-rear stripe, straight over the top of the car, that became the hallmark of Shelby Mustangs. In fact, this big, bold stripe was an option, and it seems to have been installed by Shelby; by the dealer who sold the car; or even by the buyer. There are Shelby Mustangs without the stripe, and (needless to say) there are also plenty of non-Shelby Mustangs which *do* have the stripe.

It may, of course, be that this eminently desirable car is still not radical enough for you. What do you do? Easy: upgrade it to "R" (Racing) specification.

OPPOSITE PAGE, ABOVE LEFT AND RIGHT *After testing the 428 engine in a GT500 Car and Driver commented that the car "does with ease what the old (GT350) took brute force to accomplish."*

First of all, forget about smoothness and tractability: go for raw power, and see how much you can get out of the engine. You should be able to find 350 horses cowering in the recesses of the oilways and combustion chambers; drag them out into the light. Don't forget full instrumentation (including oil temperature gauge).

This is going to be a hot-running engine, so install a larger-capacity radiator, and add an oil cooler – and install a front "apron" that directs air towards both the radiators, and the front brakes. Nor are the front brakes the only ones that are going to run hot, so install additional scoops to cool the rear brakes as well.

Power-to-weight ratios involve weight as well as power, so add some more lightness by installing Plexiglas (methyl methacrylate) rear and side windows, and substitute sliding windows for the wind-up windows in the door.

To get the power on the road use 15 x 7-inch mag wheels, and to keep the engine well supplied with fuel (for it will be prodigiously thirsty), put a 32-gallon tank in the trunk; equip it with a really big mouth, for rapid fuelling in the middle of a race. Get the fuel to the engine with an electric fuel pump: less reliable than a mechanical pump, maybe, but able to deliver fuel in the quantities the engine will require.

Finally, because mishaps do happen, add a roll bar, proper over-the-shoulder harness, and a fire extinguisher, and make sure that

ABOVE AND RIGHT *By 1967 Ford was putting more emphasis on styling than on performance. They were also adamant that the Shelbys be profitable.*

the interior is as flame-proof as possible. At this point, you will have a GT350R.

With hindsight, it is incredible that only 37 GT350R Mustangs were built in 1965, out of a total of only 562 Shelby Mustangs. Why did nobody see what Carroll Shelby was making? But such is history.

Unfortunately, Ford's bean-counters were unhappy with Shelby Mustang sales. Instead of seeing the GT350 as the finest advertising they could get, they saw it as just another car, which had to pay its way.

TOP AND ABOVE, OPPOSITE PAGE TOP AND BOTTOM *The Shelby logo in various guises is still unmistakable.*

Accordingly, the limited slip differential and the Koni shocks were made options, instead of stock items; the spring rates were softened; the Sidewinder-style exhausts were replaced with conventionally-exiting exhausts with normal mufflers (a modification that was already standard in cars intended for California, Florida and New Jersey); and in the course of the year, first the modified suspension was deleted, and then the over-the-axle traction bars, the latter to be replaced with under-the-axle bars which were cheaper to install. Most cars had stock rear seats, and some had steel hoods. Even the wood-rim steering wheel became an option, with a wood-grain plastic wheel replacing it as standard, and the battery was no longer relocated to the trunk. The only things on the bright side were the substitution of rear windows for the standard extractor louvres, and the standardization of functional rear brake-cooling scoops on all models (except for the six convertibles, where it would have interfered with the hood mechanism).

It seemed, therefore, that the Ford marketing men were locked in a very traditional, simplistic mind-set; and this was confirmed by the availability of a Paxton supercharger, which gave still better straight-line acceleration, even though many of the handling subtleties of the 1965 models had gone by the board. Worst of all, another option was a 3-speed slush-box; if you bought this, you also got a 600 cfm Ford carburetor instead of the proper Holley 715. The 1966 Shelby Mustang was still a very fine Mustang; but no longer was it a purist's car.

Ford's marketing decisions were vindicated by sales, which rose to 2,380 – a figure which was considerably inflated by the purchase of 1,000 Shelby Mustangs by Hertz, for use as hire cars. To an enthusiast, though, it looked (and still looks) like a classic example of short-sightedness. If Rolls Royce brought out a $10,000 compact tomorrow, they would sell like hot cakes simply because they had the Rolls Royce name on them. But as soon as Rolls Royce compacts became

There was, however, some good news. The roll bar was standard, and inertia-reel seat belts made their first-ever appearance on an American car. More significantly, while the 306 bhp engine remained the base unit, two bigger engines were made available. One was the short-lived 427, which has already been described elsewhere: Ford's homologation special racing engine, with forged crank and rods, forged pistons, mechanical valve actuation and a higher compression ratio, fed by two Holley 652 cfm carburreters mounted on a "dual-quad" intake. This spectacular engine was rated at 425 bhp, and the 47 Mustangs in which it was used were the most powerful Mustangs ever built.

The cars with the 427 cid engine were designated GT500, apparently as a nice round number that differentiated them from the GT350, and the same GT500 designation was used for Mustangs equipped with the altogether less impressive (though still mighty) 428 cid engine, which was rated at a mere (!) 355 bhp. The carburation of both engines was interesting, though: in normal

commonplace, the name would cease to mean anything. This, apparently, was the path to which Ford wished to commit themselves with the Shelby Mustangs.

By 1967, the familiar trend became even more pronounced. Instead of being a car which looked very much like a standard Mustang, but went very much more quickly, the Shelby became more of a styling exercise: Ford seemed to use the car as a test-bed for ideas which would appear later on the more ordinary production cars, a standard marketing ploy where this year's deluxe model becomes next year's ordinary model, while a new super-deluxe model with still more features replaces it at the top of the line. The main styling difference between Shelby Mustangs and regular Mustangs was the generous use of glass-reinforced plastic at the front end, to create an even more aggressive appearance: there was also a ducktail spoiler, and tail-lights from the Cougar.

driving, only the two primary barrels of the front carburetter were used, but under hard acceleration, fuel was supplied not only by the two secondary barrels of the front carburetter, but also by all four barrels of the rear carburetter: a veritable Niagara of gasoline. Both carburetters, incidentally, were mounted "backwards" when compared with their normal orientation.

If you wanted really serious carburation, though, there was a dealer-installed option of four twin-choke (twin-barrel) Webers. They

LEFT AND BELOW *The 1967 Shelby Mustangs were in effect the last to be truly designed and shaped by Shelby. In 1968 production of Shelby Mustangs was transferred to Michigan, where A. O. Smith converted stock Mustangs into Shelbys.*

were (and are) a swine to set up, and if you used all that power, you would find that every time you drove past a gas station, they would salute you as a valued customer!

The only trouble with the 1967 GT350 and GT500 Shelby Mustangs was that they were mechanically too close to production Mustangs. No more the revised suspension, the special brakes, the carefully-tuned steering; instead, power steering was standard, and air conditioning was an option. Even the instrumentation was (fairly) standard GT, with a 140 mph speedometer and 9,000 rpm rev counter. If there had never been a 1965 GT350, the 1967 GT350 and GT500 would have been extremely fine fast touring cars; but as it was, they were a result of the familiar Ford phenomenon of trying to be all things to all men and thereby alienating the purists in the process. Also, if you pushed a 1967 too hard into a corner, you could frighten yourself silly.

In 1968, production of Shelby Mustangs became an entirely in-house operation at Ford, at the AO Smith factory in Illinois. If you suspect that this was bad news for performance-oriented Mustang buyers, you are absolutely right.

To begin with, the 306 bhp 289 engine was dropped, and the production 302 cid engine (slightly "warmed-up" to 250 bhp) became the base engine for the GT350. For the GT500, the 428 lost its dual-quad carburation, and was fed instead by a single Holley 650 cfm; but its rated power somehow rose by 5 bhp to 360 bhp. During the model year, the GT500 was replaced by the GT500KR ("King of the Road", would you believe?) which regressed to 355 bhp. Incredibly, it is also possible that some so-called GT500s are actually equipped with 390 cid engines, because Ford ran short on 428s and substituted the smaller engine, with a loss of about 75 bhp.

The acceleration of the Shelby Mustangs was still pretty dramatic (at least when equipped with the genuine 428 cid engine),

RIGHT *Big-block 428 V8s were first offered on 1967 GT500s, as pictured here. In 1968, however, a shortage of 428s meant some GT500s were fitted with ordinary 390 V8s.*

but the car had effectively changed its character completely: it was now a top-of-the-line production car, with all the comforts and luxuries of a high-quality grand tourer. It was, in fact, an excellent car. But Ford never seemed to understand a fundamental truth: if you change horses in mid-stream (from a sports Mustang to a GT Mustang), you can *never* achieve lasting credibility. You can build some very fine cars; you can sell lots of cars; but no one will take you as seriously as they should, because you will be seen as an opportunist who is more interested in a quick buck than as a manufacturer who is sincerely interested in building the best possible car for a given market.

For 1969, the Shelby Mustang was effectively an up-market, slightly restyled Mach 1 with a roll cage. It was powered by either the 290 bhp 351 cid engine or the 335 bhp 428CJ-R – and they couldn't even sell the 3,942 cars they did make, so 789 of them were

LEFT *The 1967 Shelby GT500 remains one of the great classic American sports cars.*

"updated" and sold as 1970 models. Predictably, that was the last year in which Ford attempted to sell Shelby Mustangs.

Fortunately, this sad ending – not with a bang, but a whimper – was not quite the last of the Shelby Mustang story. In 1980-1982, Carroll Shelby built a dozen 1966-specification Shelby Mustang convertibles, based on used 1966 convertibles, and numbered them continuously from the six original convertibles. To some people, these are not the real thing; but to someone who wants a car to drive, as distinct from the automotive equivalent of a stamp-collector's rarity, it is certainly not a car that most of us would be too purist to refuse to own.

Also, the success of the original Shelby Mustang illustrates a fundamental truth: the Mustang was a very good car. What was more, if you knew what you were doing, you could make all kinds of modifications which would make it an even better car.

T E C H N I C A L S P E C I F I C A T I O N	
MODEL	1965 Shelby GT350R
LENGTH	181.6 inches (4613 mm)
WIDTH	68.2 inches (1732 mm)
HEIGHT	51 inches (1295 mm)
KERB WEIGHT	2600 lb (1182 kg) approx.
WHEELBASE	108 inches (2743 mm)
TRACK	Front: 56 inches (1422 mm) Rear: 56 inches (1422 mm)
WEIGHT	Distribution (front/rear): 57/43
ENGINE	Rated bhp (SAE gross) 350 Swept volume 289 cubic inches (4736 cc) Bore 4 inches (101.6 mm) Stroke 2.87 inches (72.9 mm) Compression ratio 10.5:1 or higher
PERFORMANCE	0–60 mph Around 6 seconds Standing Quarter Around 13 seconds Top speed Around 140 mph

Modifications: limited slip differential as standard; high-rise inlet manifold; 700 cubic feet/minute Holley carburetter; custom steel exhaust manifolds; straight-through glass-pack mufflers, light-alloy oil pan and valve covers; larger radiator; oil cooler; additional instrumentation; 10.5-inch disc brakes; bigger stabilizer bar; Koni shocks, over-the-axle traction bars; braced front end; functional hood air scoop; front and rear break cooling scoops; "apron" to redirect air flow at front; relocated battery; relocated front suspension mounting; fibreglass hood; fibreglass shelf replaces rear seats; rear and side windows in Plexiglass; 32-gallon fuel tank in trunk; electric fuel pump; roll bar; competition harness; and more . . .

Note: Performance figures can vary very widely, according to the rear axle ratio chosen, the preparation of the car, weather conditions, and the mechanical sympathy (or otherwise) of the driver.

THE OTHER MUSTANGS

Early in the book, I said that some Mustang *aficionados* are obsessed with the minutiae of Ford's options list: their cars must be *exactly* according to factory specifications, otherwise they lose their "classic" status.

Hmmm.

The trouble is, these people have rather lost sight of what a Mustang – or any car for that matter – is about. First and foremost, it's a vehicle for getting about. Second, if you're lucky, it's fun.

Different people get their fun in different ways. There are some, it has to be admitted, who focus solely on the factory specification. There are others who are into the custom

BELOW *George Follmer in a Trans–Am Mustang. The Trans–Am was born at much the same time as the Mustang, and Mustangs won the first two Trans–Am series in 1966 and 1967, and then again in 1970.*

scene: if it hasn't got 18 coats of pink pearl paint, followed by enough lacquer to make it look like dawn on the horizon, they aren't interested. Some people just wanna go fast, whether in a straight line (there have been some pretty spectacular drag Mustangs) or on a race track.

For these people and many thousands of Mustang club members throughout the world, the Mustang has become almost a way of life.

The Mustang was a mass-produced vehicle, with its normal share of rattles, substitute and out-of-spec parts, paint runs and Friday-nighters. Maybe its good old nostalgia for the America of the 1960s and the freedom implied by the road movie era which

draws fans and owners alike to meetings up and down the country. Whatever the reason, these enthusiasts are motivated more by a sense of fun than financial gain or purist accuracy and thus remains true to the spirit of the original Mustangs.

There is the delicate question of what constitutes "acceptable" modifications. Are 1970s mag alloy wheels OK, but 1980s mag alloys (on a 1970s car) beyond the pale? Do you have to have Cragars, or are other makes acceptable? What about a replica Shelby free-flow exhaust system, or a medium-rise inlet manifold? Or a set of Webers, for that matter? And if Webers are acceptable (they were a dealer-installed option for some Mustangs), what about Dellortos? At one time, there used to be a hill-climb special with a Ford V8 and eight Amal motorcycle carburetters. If that car were to surface today, with modifications made more than 20 years ago, would it be a good idea to put back the 2-barrel Holley or Autolite?

The truth is, most cars tend to get modified (whether consciously or not) to suit their owners. If you are buying a Rolls Royce or a Bristol, you simply tell the gentleman who takes your order that you don't want Connolly

ABOVE *Roush is to the later Mustangs what Shelby was to the earlier ones: very, very quick, and looking it.*

RIGHT *For those unafraid to deviate from factory spec equipment, custom Mustangs can be colorful and fun.*

leather or Bedford cloth; you've always had this weakness for chamois, or raw silk. No problem. But when you buy a Mustang, you are ultimately limited to Ford's (admittedly extensive) option list; and if you want something that Mr Ford has not seen fit to offer, you can either live with the omission, or "customize" the car. It can be something as modest as a new radio or some fancy wheels, or it can be a complete Shelby-style make-over.

The "authenticity" of conversions is something that some people get very excited about, but as far as I am concerned, I'd rather have a $5,000 motor car that was fun to drive, instead of a $25,000 motor car that I was

afraid of getting scratched! If you want a 1965 Shelby, for example, your choices are fairly simple. Either you wait until you find the car you want, and then pay out very large sums of money; or you find a good 1965 bodyshell, and with a combination of money and labor, you "Shelbyize" it. When you've finished, it isn't a real Shelby and it isn't worth as much as a real Shelby; but what were you trying for, a collector's item, or a car to drive?

Obviously, the extent to which it is appropriate to modify any car depends on its rarity. For example, turning a GT500 into a custom low-rider would be very foolish, because you could equally well start out with a very much cheaper Mustang, and you would be knocking thousands off the value as you modified it. But the vast majority of Mustangs are not that rare, and modifying them – even modifying them radically – does not fall into the realm of heresy. The pictures in this chapter are pictures that either I or the picture researcher could not resist. They show what can be done with the Mustang, and what some people have done with the Mustang. If you are modifying your own Mustang, I hope you find them an inspiration.

As we have already seen, the history of the Mustang began with a bang; ran like a greyhound for a couple of years; wallowed about uncertainly for more than a decade; and then began to harden into classicism, an American sports car which is as archetypal in its way as a Morgan or a Ferrari. No one can predict how much longer the Ford Mustang will last: given the past record of FoMoCo, it might be canceled tomorrow, or it might run into the twenty-first century.

LEFT *Several drivers have campaigned Mustang "funny cars" of various types, and (like Mustangs modified for more conventional motor sports), Micky Thompson's Mach 1 was very successful.*

FAR LEFT *This 1971 Mach 1 Mustang features a Ford Cleveland 351 cid engine and Holley 3310-2 carburettor.*

LEFT *Show-room condition Mustangs are hard to find and costly when you do. This 1967 bespoilered fastback looks immaculate.*

Gone are the days when a Mustang was the ultimate American "muscle car", the epitome of brute power. There are many cars which are more powerful than even the fastest modern Mustang, and not a few that are more brutal, too.

Even so, a Mustang remains desirable. Partly, it is an echo of a time that is gone: a time of fast cars and skinny tires and insufficient brakes, but a lot of *brio*. Partly too, it is a fast, modern touring car which is at home on the way to the shops, or as the star of the Road Movie (and which *does* have adequate tires and brakes). Which Mustang you buy will depend on how you see yourself, and on how you want others to see you. But if you don't try at least one Mustang, at least once – and you have over a quarter of a century of model years to choose from – you will never quite understand one of the motoring legends of the second half of the twentieth century.

Index

Picture Credits

All pictures were supplied by Ford Motor Company of Detroit, Michigen except:
Trevor Wood – pp 1, 2
Classic American – pp 103 top, 108 all, 110–1 all, 116, 113 all, 114–5 all, 116
Mike Key – pp 13, 29 top, 122, 123
Mustang Monthly – pp 22–3, 46–7, 56–7, 78–9
R Walkden – pp 119 bottom